I am *worthy* of love & respect.

A GUIDED JOURNAL FOR SELF-LOVE & CLARITY

Allyson Leak

AMETHYST
LIFE

Published by Amethyst Life, LLC

Editor: Audrey Leak Coates

ATTENTION NON-PROFITS
Books are available at a discount with bulk orders for educational use. Please contact allyson.leak@amethystlife.com.

The information provided in this book is for educational purposes and is not intended as a substitute for professional medical or psychological advice.

The author and publisher disclaim any responsibility for any liability, loss, or risk, personal or otherwise, which may be incurred as a consequence, directly or indirectly, from using and applying any content in this book. Readers are advised to use their judgment and discretion to interpret and utilize the information provided.

This journal is intended for individuals seeking self-improvement and personal growth.

ISBN: 979-8-9896010-1-1

Printed in the United States of America

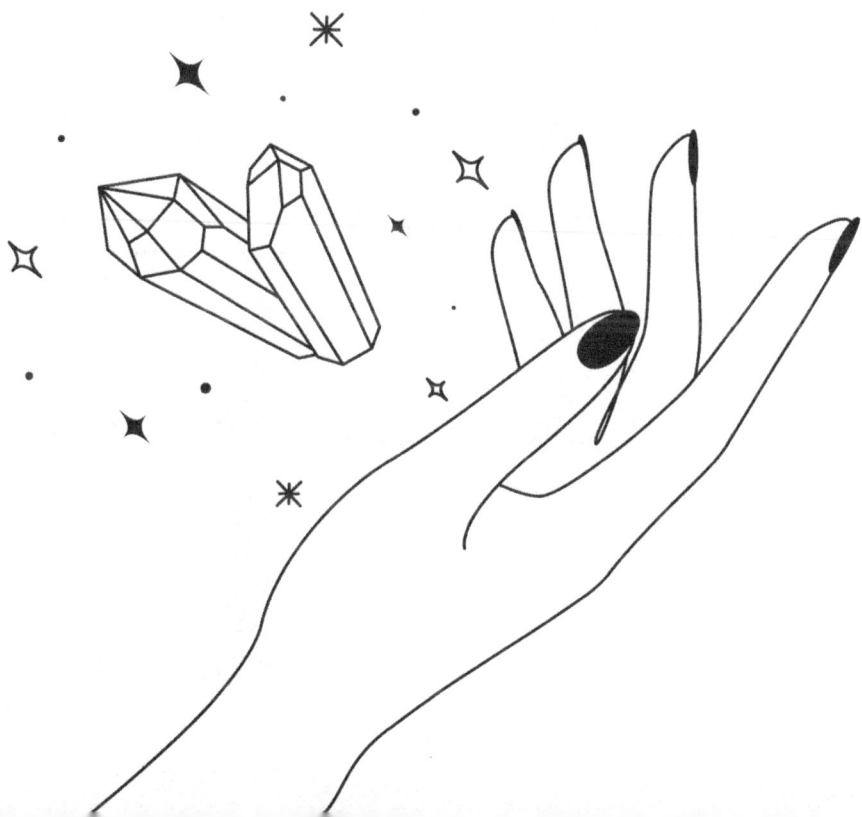

SELF

LOVE

THIS JOURNAL BELONGS TO

I activate
peace, love,
and
abundance in
my life ♡

LIFE IS A JOURNEY

Life is an incredible journey, and journaling is such a beautiful way to reflect on important moments. I've found writing to be therapeutic and such an amazing form of self-care. It truly feels like a creative outlet for my soul. Journaling helps me process my thoughts, find my center, and cultivate awareness about my desires and needs. It helps build self-awareness, which is the first step towards real change and growth. I have twelve journals. Some are small and portable, while four are massive, towering up to my knee. They're filled with my thoughts on life, its ups and downs, my future plans, and spiritual insights. I use certain entries as prayers, which has also deepened my relationship with God, and I am so thankful for that.

Nowadays, it's so easy to get lost in the whirlwind of daily life. This journal is meant to be your sanctuary—a pause button for reflection and growth. It's lovingly crafted with prompts and creative activities to bring balance and inner peace into your life. Practicing self-love and gaining clarity through journaling can profoundly impact how you perceive yourself and the world, which can help you foster self-respect. Try to find a realistic time and space for journaling. Whether in a serene room or accompanied by calming music, remember to take a moment to center yourself before you begin. Keep it simple, go at your own pace, and always be gentle with yourself.

I wish you all the best!

Love & Light.
Allyson

Journaling BENEFITS

Improved Emotional Well-Being:
Journaling has been found to reduce symptoms of depression and anxiety. Writing about emotions or about any traumatic experiences you have faced can help you process and make sense of your feelings and, as a result, lead to improved mental health.

Stress Reduction:
Rumination, or repeatedly thinking about the same negative thoughts, contributes to stress. Research shows that expressive writing can reduce anxiety and improve overall psychological well-being. Journaling helps break this cycle by externalizing thoughts onto paper.

Enhanced Cognitive Function:
Regular journaling can boost cognitive function. It can improve memory, problem-solving skills, and critical thinking. It can also help you organize your thoughts and clarify your ideas.

Better Self-Awareness:
By reflecting on your thoughts and emotions, you better understand yourself, your goals, and your values. This self-awareness can lead to clarity and personal growth and help you establish a habit of seeking out and appreciating the good things in your life.

LIVING WELL

Here is a list of ideas that can contribute to a healthy lifestyle.

for Clarity

Morning Meditation: Start the day with at least ten minutes to clear the mind and set intentions. Sit comfortably, focus on your breath, and allow thoughts to pass without judgment. This helps bring mental clarity and reduces stress.

Journaling for Reflection: Spend time each day journaling to reflect on your thoughts, feelings, and experiences. This practice helps to sort through emotions, gain insight, and organize ideas.

De-cluttering Space: You can make your space sacred by allocating monthly time to de-clutter and organize. Whether it's your home, workspace, or personal areas, removing unnecessary items, organizing belongings, and creating an ordered space can promote a clearer mind and enhance focus and productivity.

Nature Walks: Being in natural environments, such as parks, forests, or near bodies of water, has a calming effect on the mind. Spending time in nature has been linked to a reduction in anxiety and stress hormones. Fresh air contains higher oxygen levels than indoor air; better oxygen intake can enhance concentration and clarity of mind.

Digital Detox: Try to spend a few hours disconnected from electronic devices each week. Do something that helps you unwind. You could read, paint, or spend time with loved ones. Disconnecting from technology can declutter the mind.

Mindful Breathing: Incorporate specific breathing exercises or mindful breathing techniques into your daily routine. Spend a few minutes in the morning practicing deep, intentional breathing, focusing solely on inhalation and exhalation.

Gratitude: Reflect on blessings, accomplishments, or positive aspects of life. This practice can shift focus toward positivity and increase overall happiness.

for Self-Care

Self-Compassion Practice: Dedicate time to self-compassion exercises, such as positive affirmations, self-appreciation, or listening to a self-love meditation. This can remind you to be gentle with yourself along life's journey.

Bubble Baths or Relaxing Soaks: Take time for a relaxing bath with essential oils, bath bombs, or Epsom salts. This ritual helps relax muscles, reduces tension, and promotes a sense of calm. You can also recite your affirmations while in the bath, too. If you can't take a bath, try a weekly foot soak.

Healthy Eating and Mindful Nutrition: Focus on nourishing your body with nutritious meals. Cook or prepare food mindfully, paying attention to flavors and textures. You can set a relaxing mood with good music or listen to an audiobook while cooking.

Establishing Boundaries: Try to practice setting boundaries in professional and personal relationships. Don't be afraid to say no to something that doesn't feel right in your spirit. Prioritizing self-care and communicating your needs clearly can reduce stress. It is how you keep your mind, body, and soul safe.

Prayer: Set aside a specific time for prayer. This will help deepen your connection to God and focus on gratitude, guidance, and inner peace. This practice can calm the mind, provide spiritual nourishment, and contribute to inner harmony.

Creative Expression: Engage in a creative activity that brings you joy, whether painting, writing, crafting, jewelry making, or any other form of creative expression. Allowing yourself time for creativity promotes relaxation.

Guided Meditation: Whether daily, once a week, or once a month, find time to add regular meditation to your life. Try incorporating regular guided meditation or mindfulness practice sessions into your self-care routine. Meditation aids in reducing stress and enhancing self-awareness.

You are loved and cherished beyond your wildest dreams!

MY
intention for this journal

_____

_____

_____

_____

.

> ## MY FAVORITE QUOTE IS

ABOUT ME

I am beautiful, unique, and important!

MEANING OF MY NAME

FAVORITE COLOR

FAVORITE SEASON

FAVORITE ACTIVITY

THE DAILY GOAL, THE MAGIC 3

The Magic 3 represents the three core emotions you aim to experience daily.

By delving into these feelings and recognizing the individuals and environments that evoke these emotions within you, you can use this framework to prioritize your time and activities. What are the three emotions you aspire to feel each day?

1. _____

2. _____

3. _____

WORDS FOR INSPIRATION...

THE DAILY GOAL

What does each word you chose for the Magic 3
mean to you?

#1

#2

#3

THE PEOPLE

List three people that make you feel like your Magic 3 and why they do.

THE THINGS

List three things or activities that make you feel like your Magic 3.

THE ENVIRONMENT

List three places that make you feel like your Magic 3.

MOOD BOARD

Paste pictures of things that make you feel good.

inspiration.

What does self-love mean to you?
Reflect on a time when you showed
yourself love. Describe the impact it
had on your well-being.

_____

_____

_____

_____

_____

_____

_____

_____

_____

_____

_____

_____

_____

_____

_____

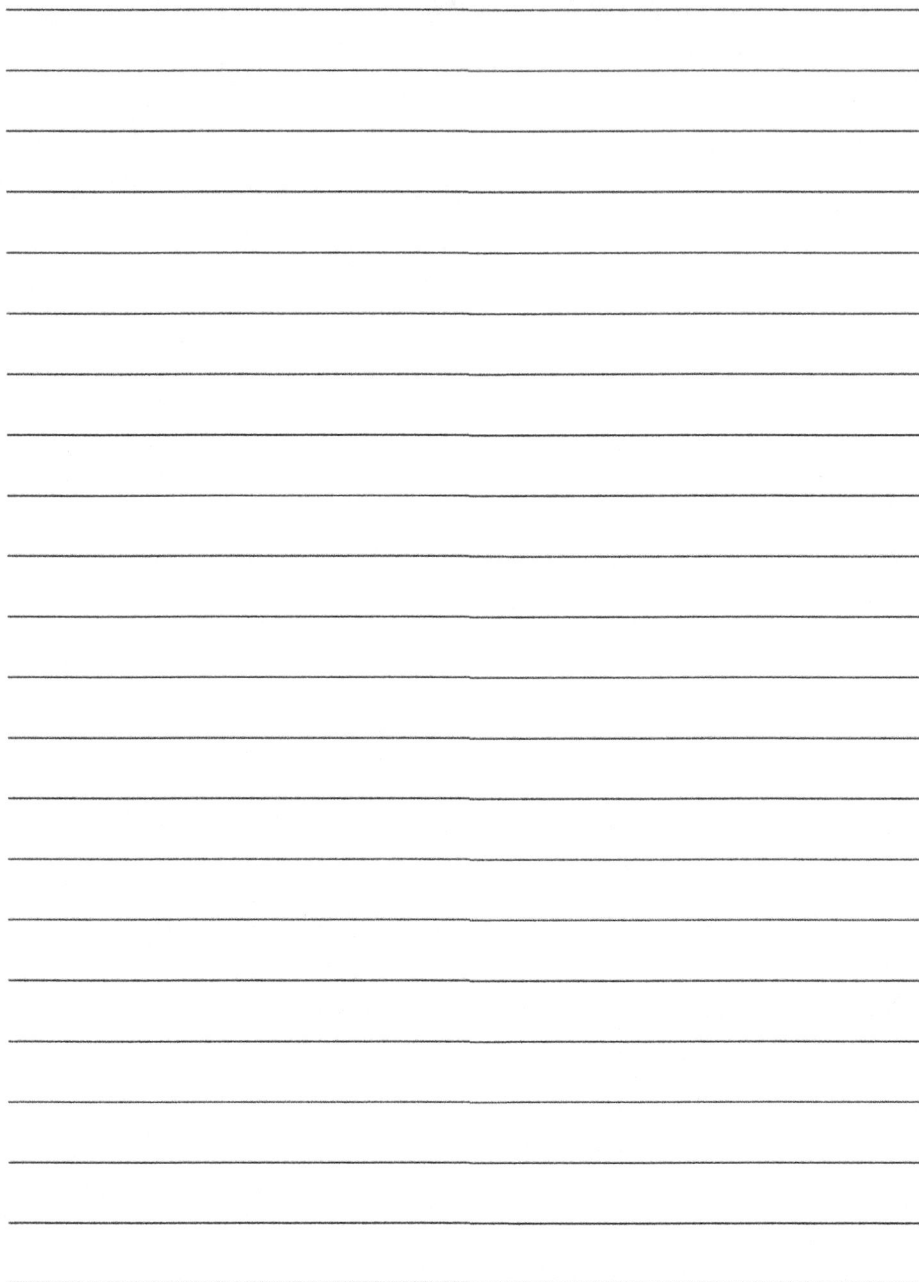

Write a letter to your future self about
the importance of self-love. Include
advice that will continue to guide you   DATE
on your path toward fulfillment.

_____

_____

_____

_____

_____

_____

_____

_____

_____

_____

_____

_____

_____

_____

_____

_____

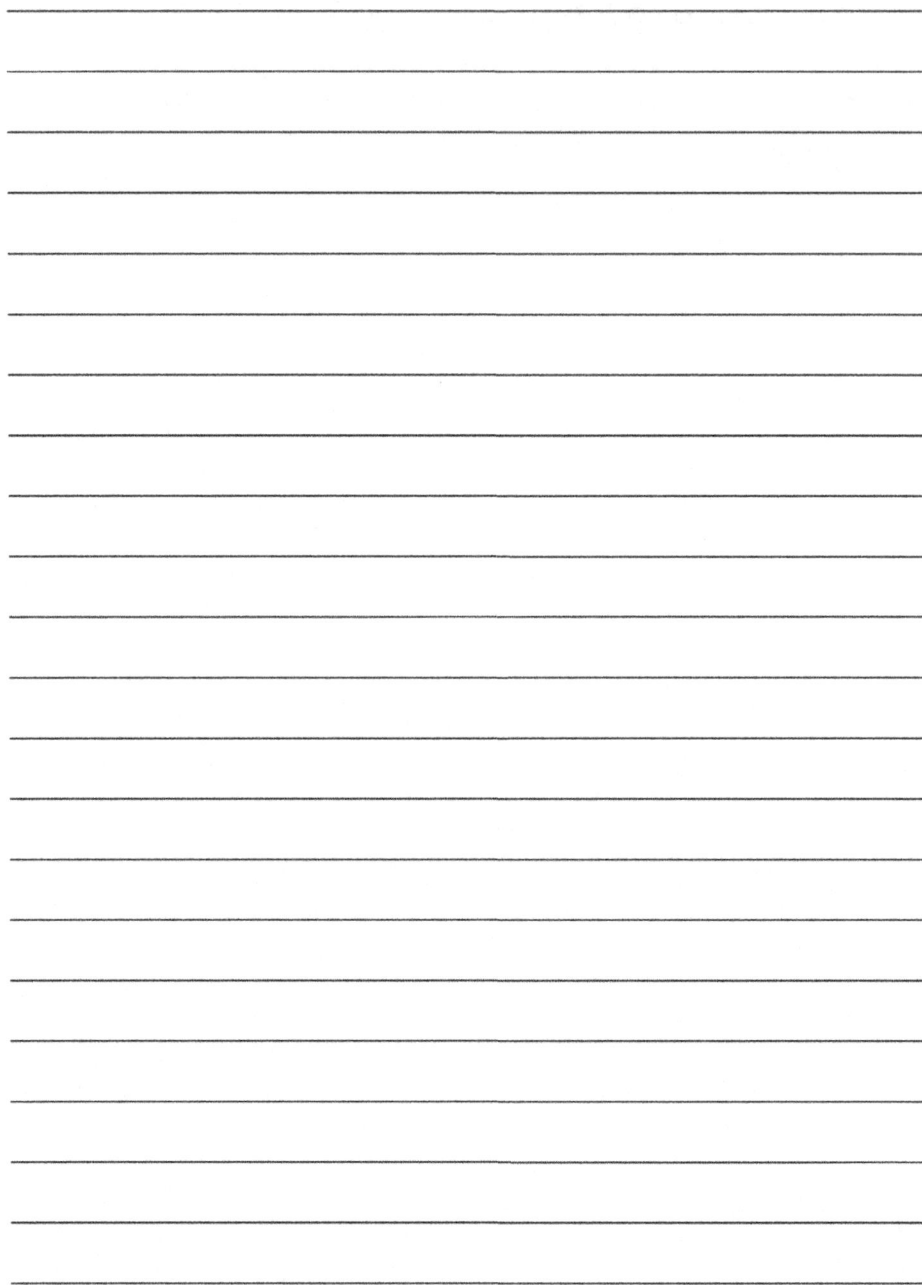

List your favorite shows or movies that help lift your spirits, and then explain why they do.

DATE _____

_____

_____

_____

_____

_____

_____

_____

_____

_____

_____

_____

_____

_____

_____

_____

_____

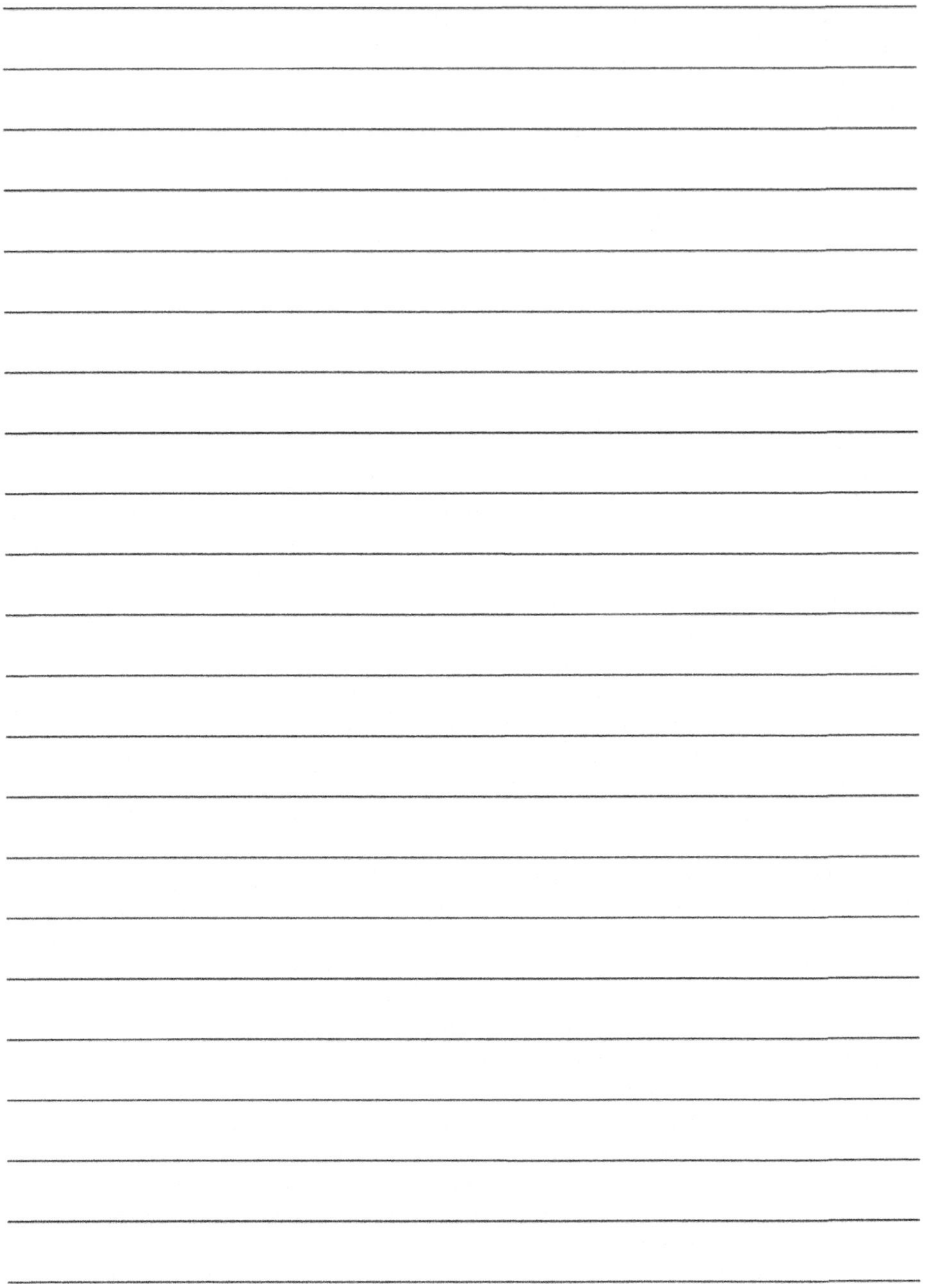

List eight things you love about
yourself and why.

_____

_____

_____

_____

_____

_____

_____

_____

_____

_____

_____

_____

_____

_____

_____

_____

_____

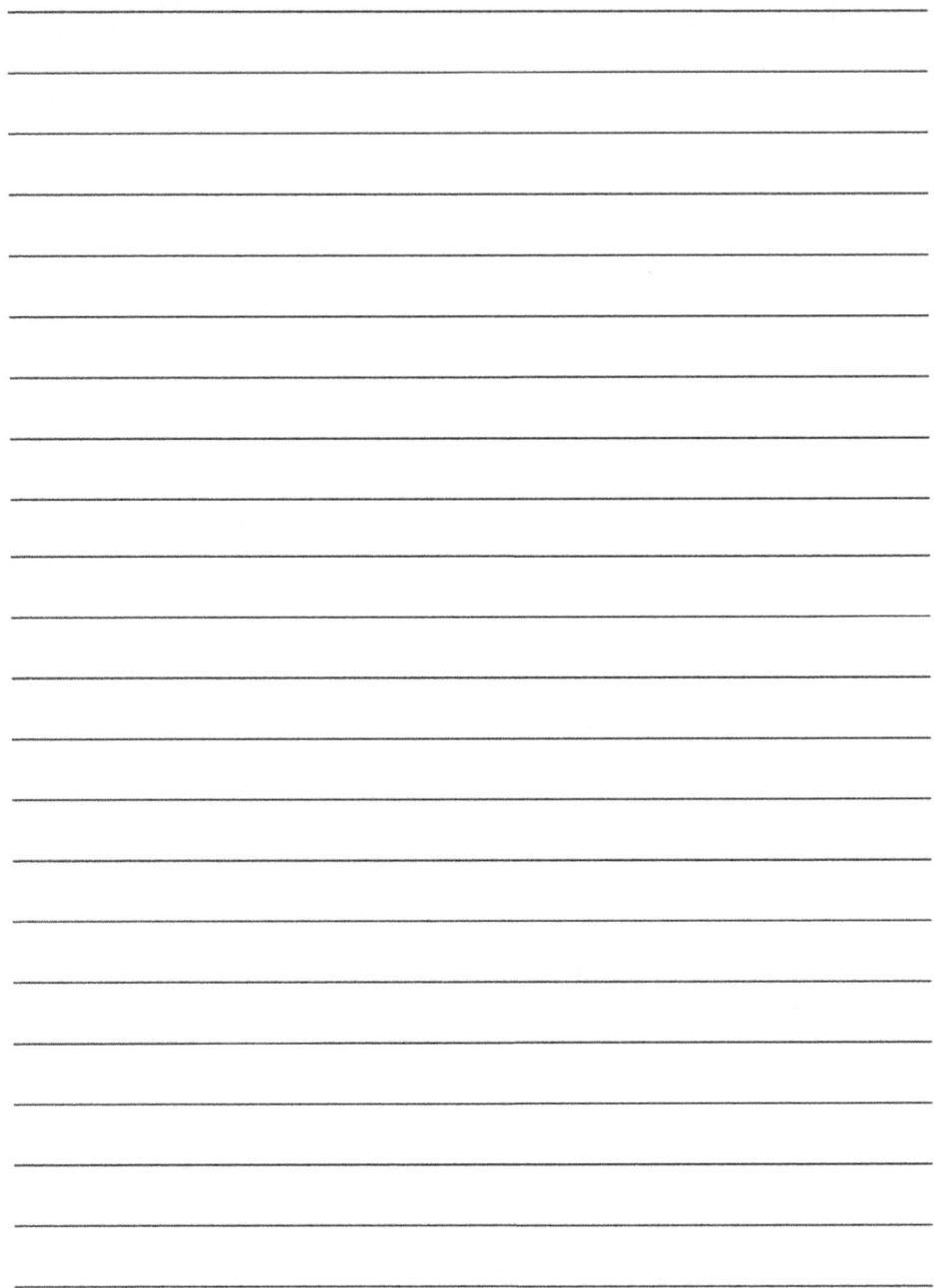

Describe a time when you felt truly confident in yourself. Describe the circumstances and the emotions you felt.

DATE _____

_____

_____

_____

_____

_____

_____

_____

_____

_____

_____

_____

_____

_____

_____

_____

_____

_____

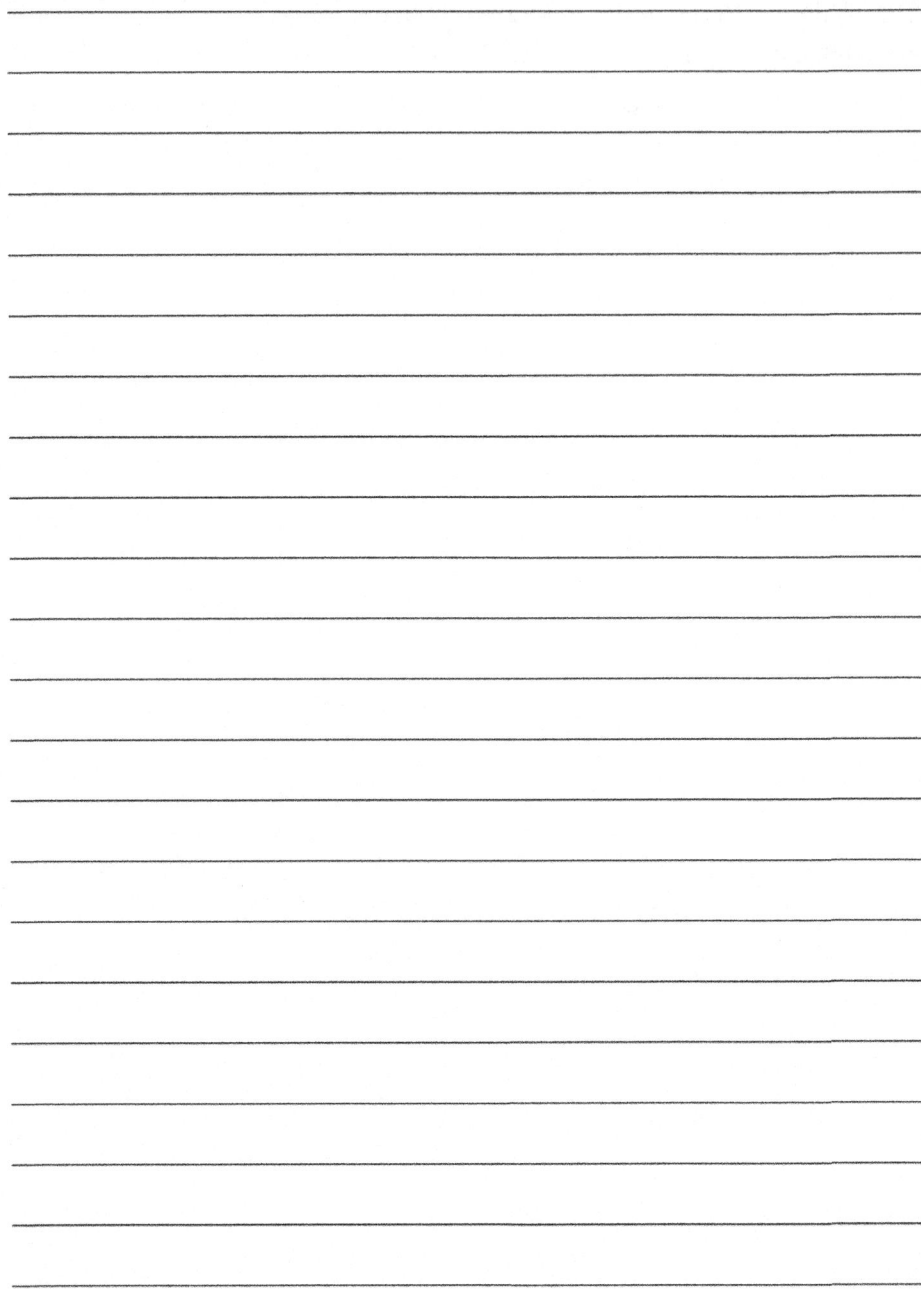

BE GENTLE
WITH
YOURSELF

LIST IDEAS FOR SELF-CARE

PHYSICAL SELF-CARE

-
-
-

EMOTIONAL SELF-CARE

-
-
-

SPIRITUAL SELF-CARE

-
-
-

INTELLECTUAL SELF-CARE

-
-
-

SOCIAL SELF-CARE

-
-
-

FINANCIAL SELF-CARE

-
-
-

What are your core values and
beliefs? Do they come from your
upbringing, personal experiences,
or influential figures in your life?

DATE _____

_____

_____

_____

_____

_____

_____

_____

_____

_____

_____

_____

_____

_____

_____

_____

_____

_____

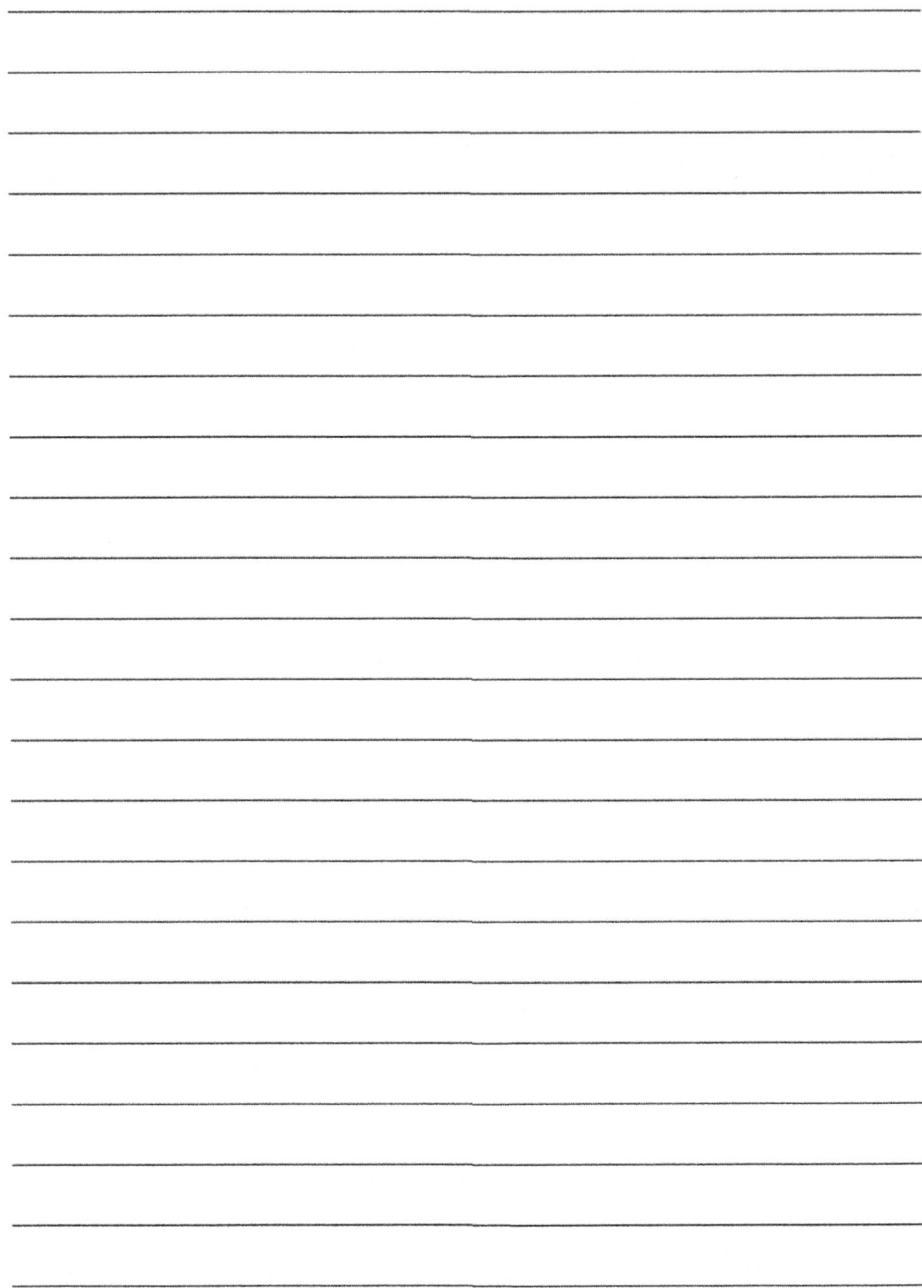

Identify any negative self-talk or
limiting beliefs. Where does it come
from? How can you reframe these
thoughts?

_____

_____

_____

_____

_____

_____

_____

_____

_____

_____

_____

_____

_____

_____

_____

_____

_____

_____

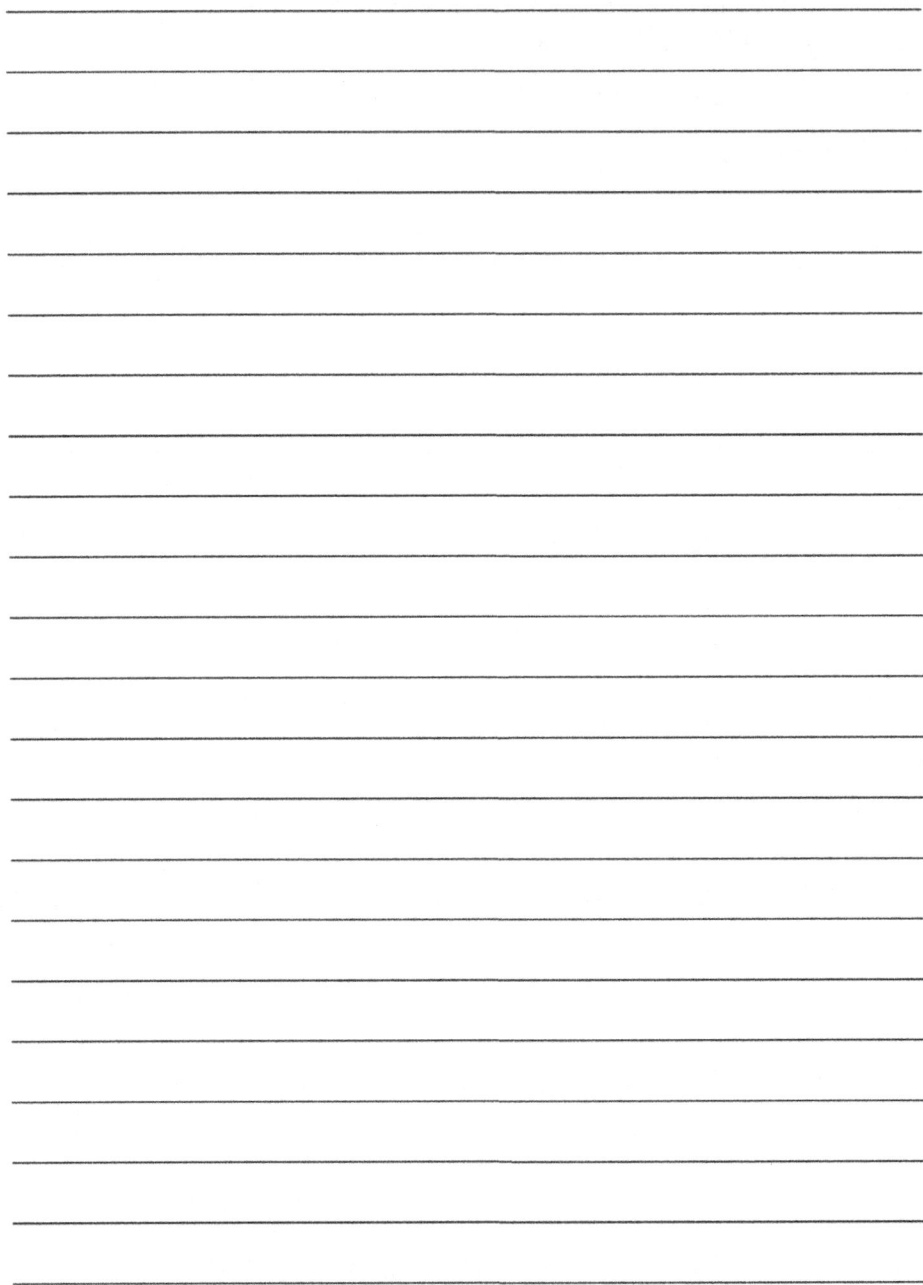

Describe a moment when you felt completely at peace. Did it stem from an external environment, such as nature, or a state of mind?

DATE _____

_____

_____

_____

_____

_____

_____

_____

_____

_____

_____

_____

_____

_____

_____

_____

_____

_____

_____

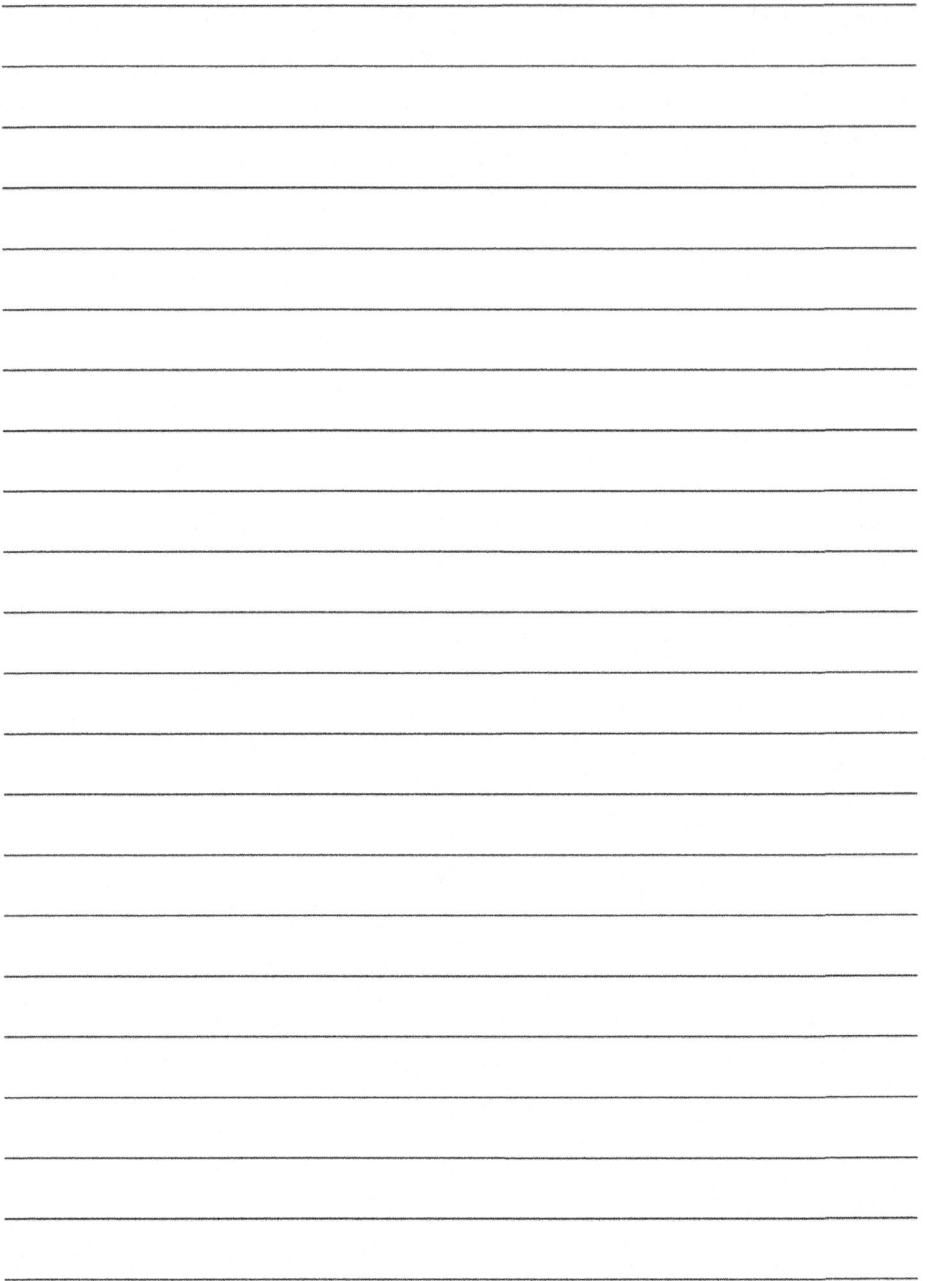

What are your favorite self-care practices? What has been working well for you? What do you think you will change?

DATE _____

_____

_____

_____

_____

_____

_____

_____

_____

_____

_____

_____

_____

_____

_____

_____

_____

_____

_____

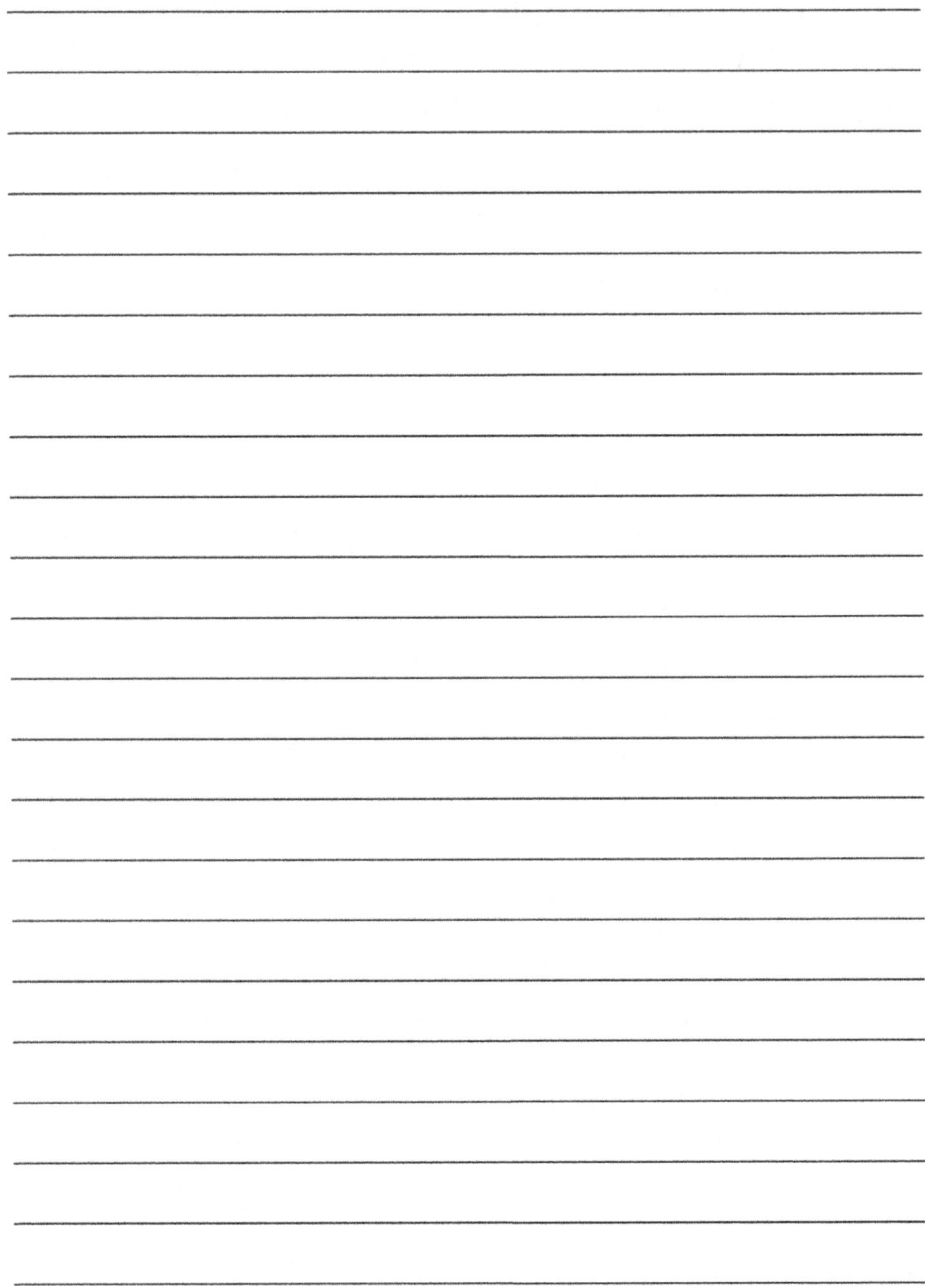

Reflect on a time when your intuition was correct. How did you feel? What signals in your body and mind gave you the hunch?

DATE _____

_____

_____

_____

_____

_____

_____

_____

_____

_____

_____

_____

_____

_____

_____

_____

_____

Creative drawing

Creative drawing

Reflect on a challenging experience that helped you grow. Describe the circumstances, lessons learned, and coping mechanisms that helped.

_____

_____

_____

_____

_____

_____

_____

_____

_____

_____

_____

_____

_____

_____

_____

_____

_____

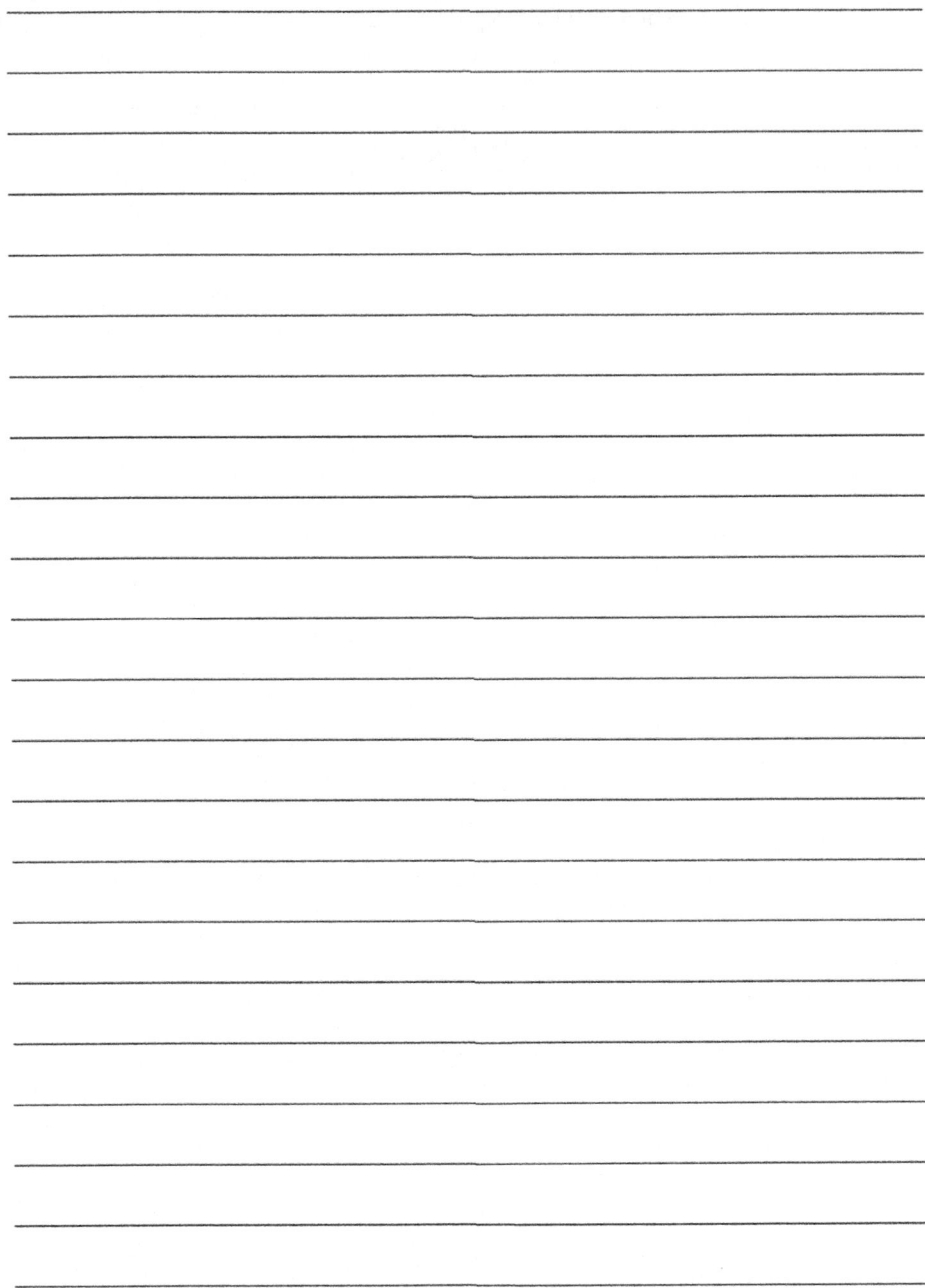

How do you handle constructive criticism? Describe your initial emotional reactions. Identify four strategies and tools to help.

DATE _____

_____

_____

_____

_____

_____

_____

_____

_____

_____

_____

_____

_____

_____

_____

_____

_____

_____

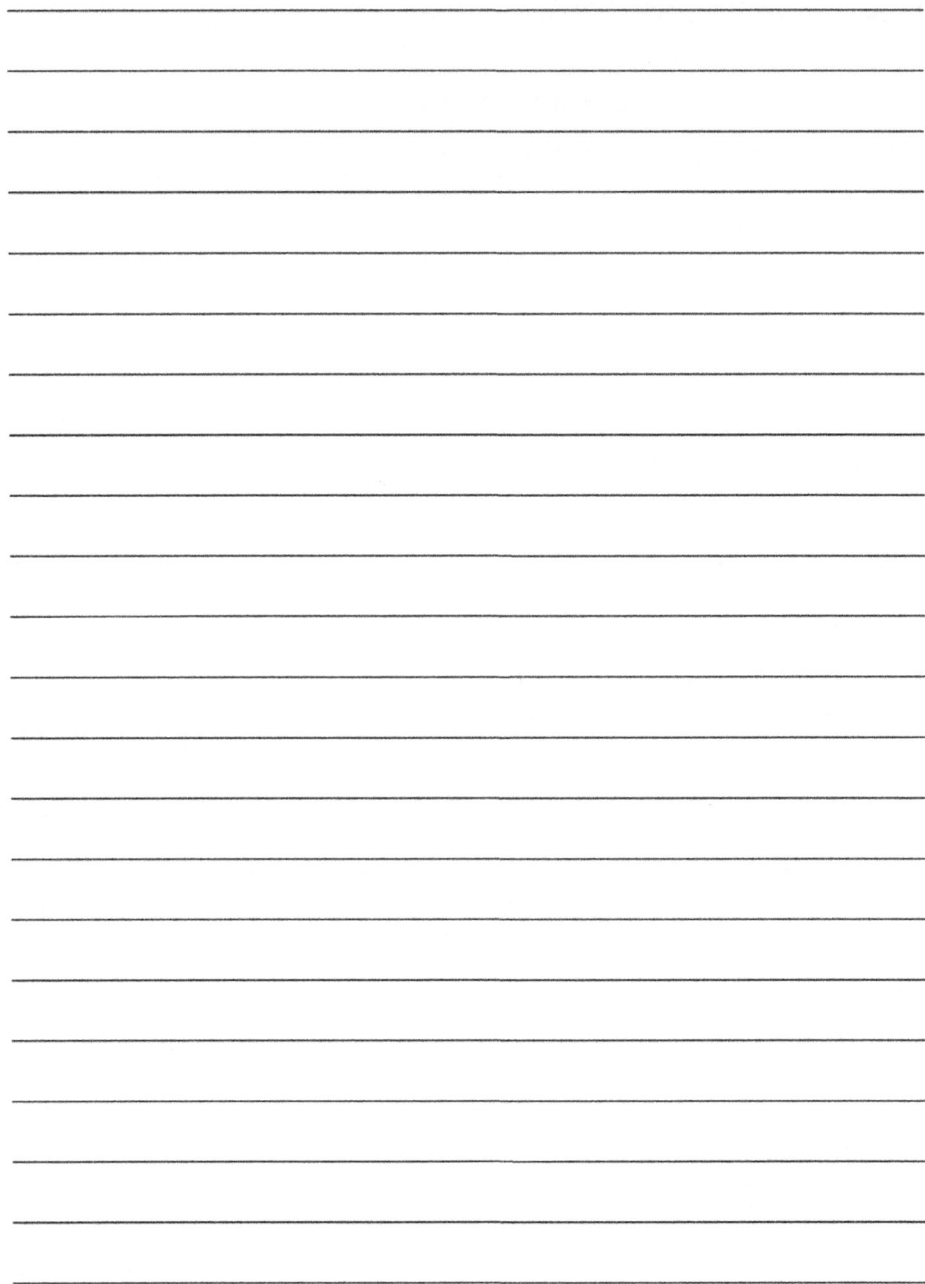

What are your talents and strengths? What are ways to further nurture and develop these attributes?

DATE _____

_____

_____

_____

_____

_____

_____

_____

_____

_____

_____

_____

_____

_____

_____

_____

_____

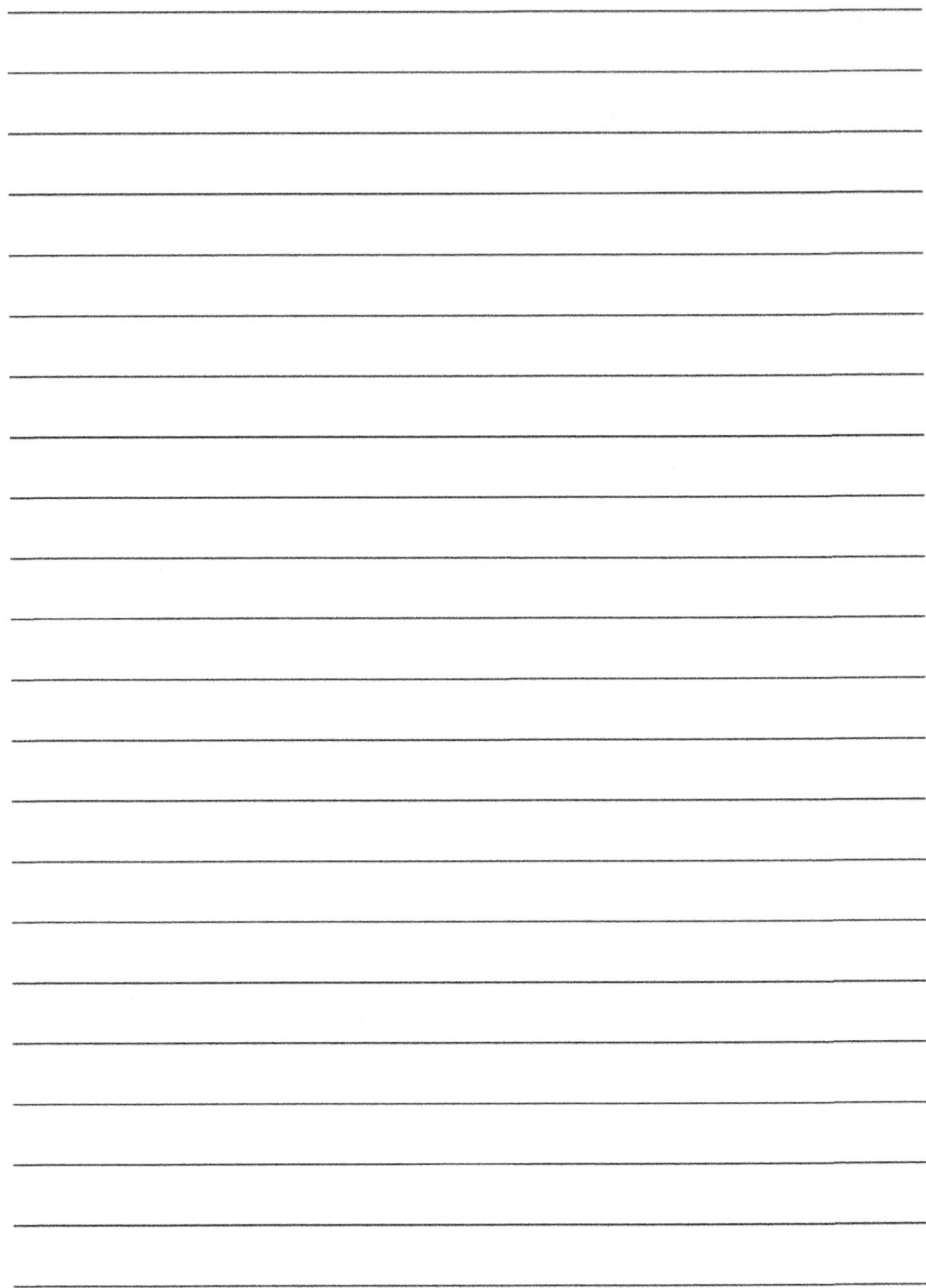

Write about a person or a situation
that has positively influenced your
self-esteem.

DATE _____

_____

_____

_____

_____

_____

_____

_____

_____

_____

_____

_____

_____

_____

_____

_____

_____

_____

_____

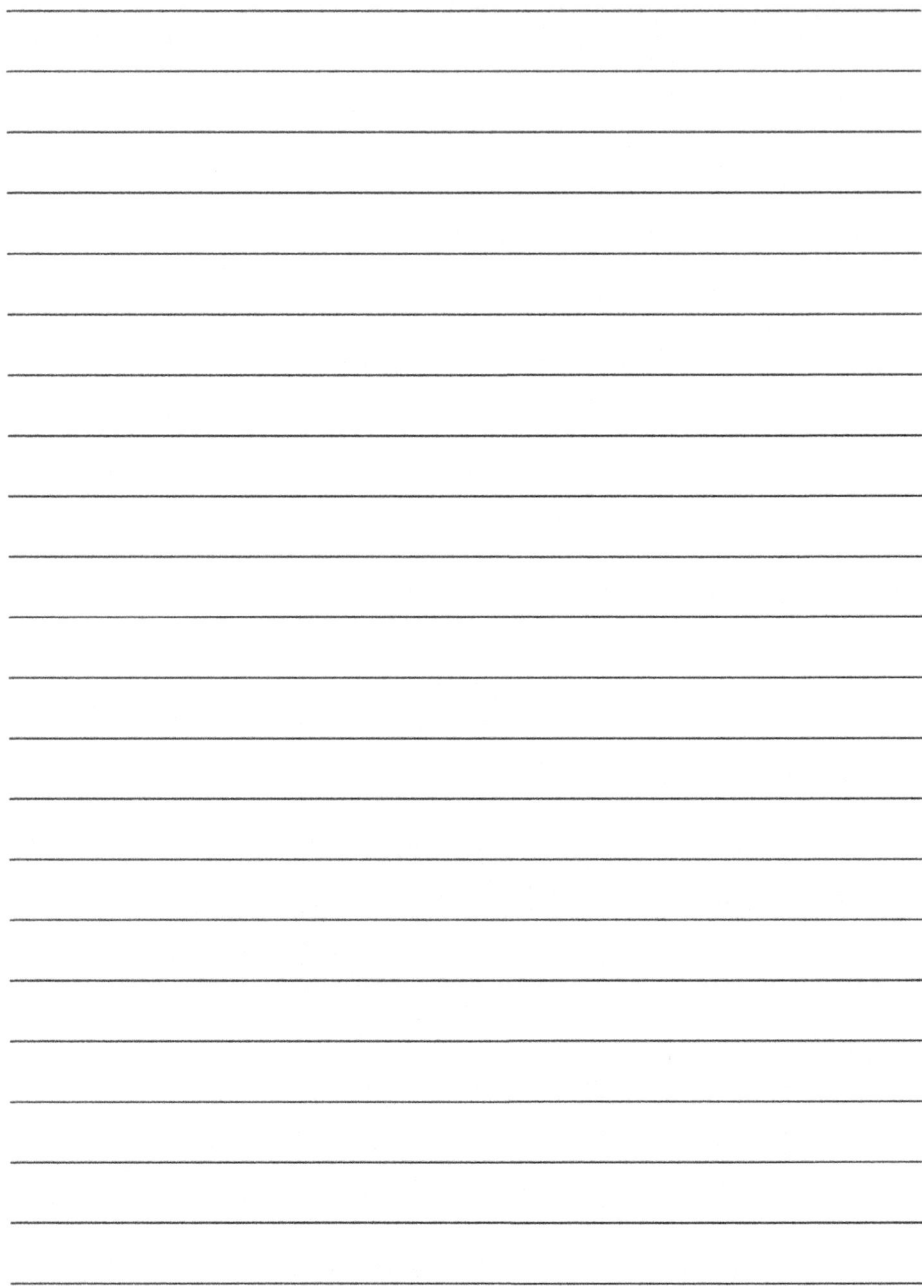

How can you prioritize self-love in your daily routine? Reflect on easy ways to incorporate self-love alongside existing habits.

DATE _____

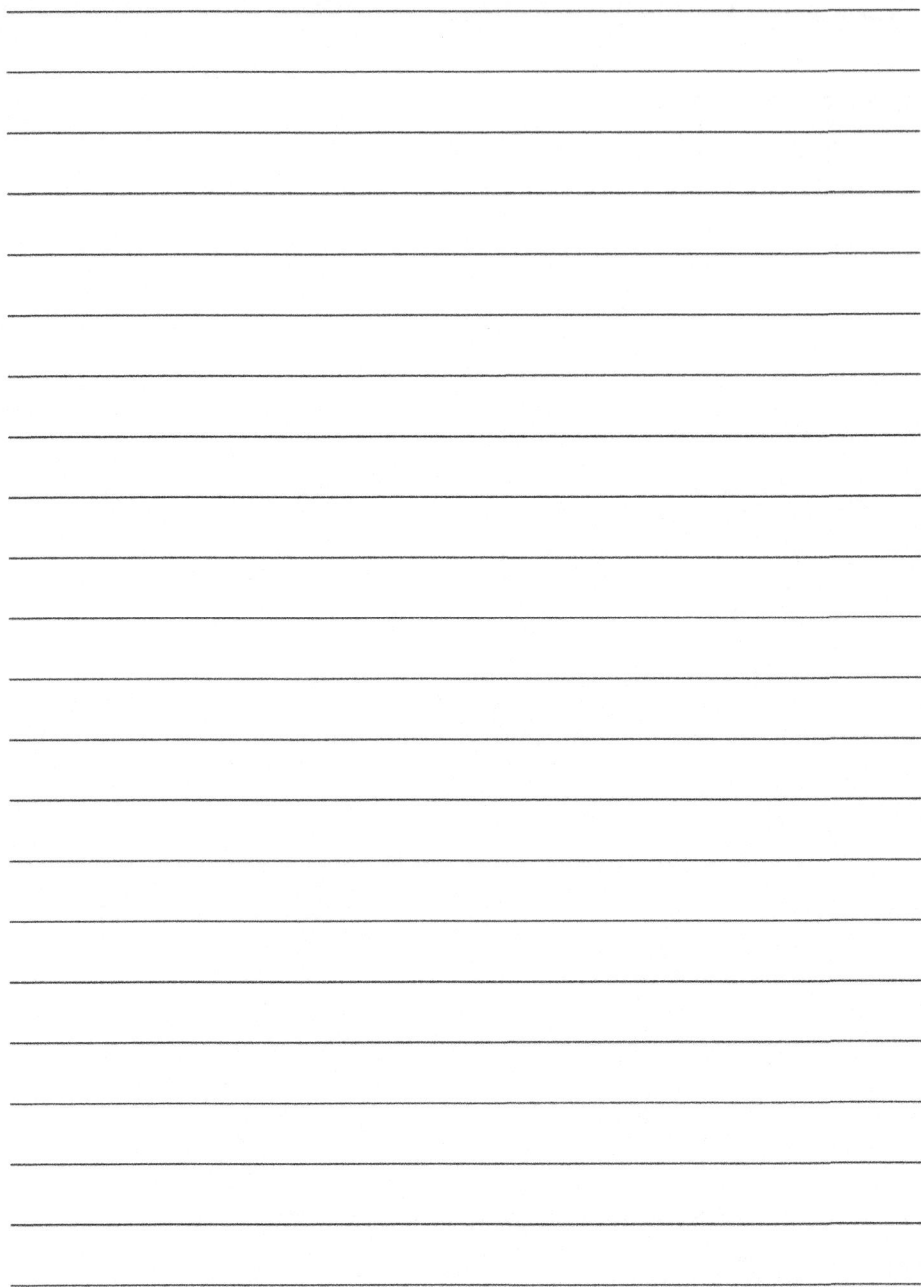

When you get to a crossroads, follow your heart, allow your inner truth to lead you.

Create an Undo List

List things or habits that you feel are no longer serving your greatest good.

1 _____

2 _____

3 _____

4 _____

5 _____

6 _____

7 _____

8 _____

Are there any obstacles that hinder
your self-love journey? Reflect on
how these hurdles have impacted

your well-being.

_____

_____

_____

_____

_____

_____

_____

_____

_____

_____

_____

_____

_____

_____

_____

_____

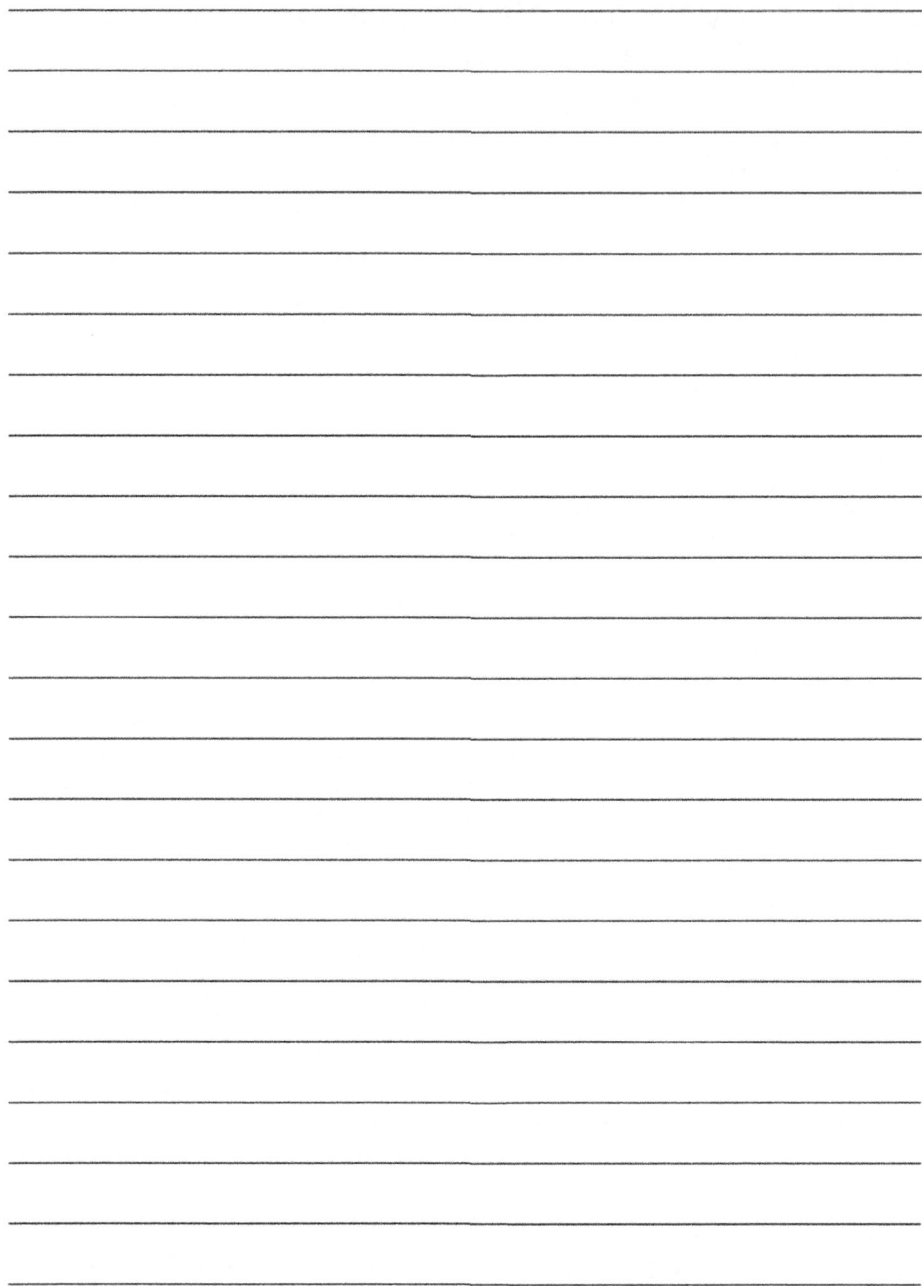

Describe a situation where you
overcame self-doubt.

DATE _____

_____

_____

_____

_____

_____

_____

_____

_____

_____

_____

_____

_____

_____

_____

_____

_____

_____

_____

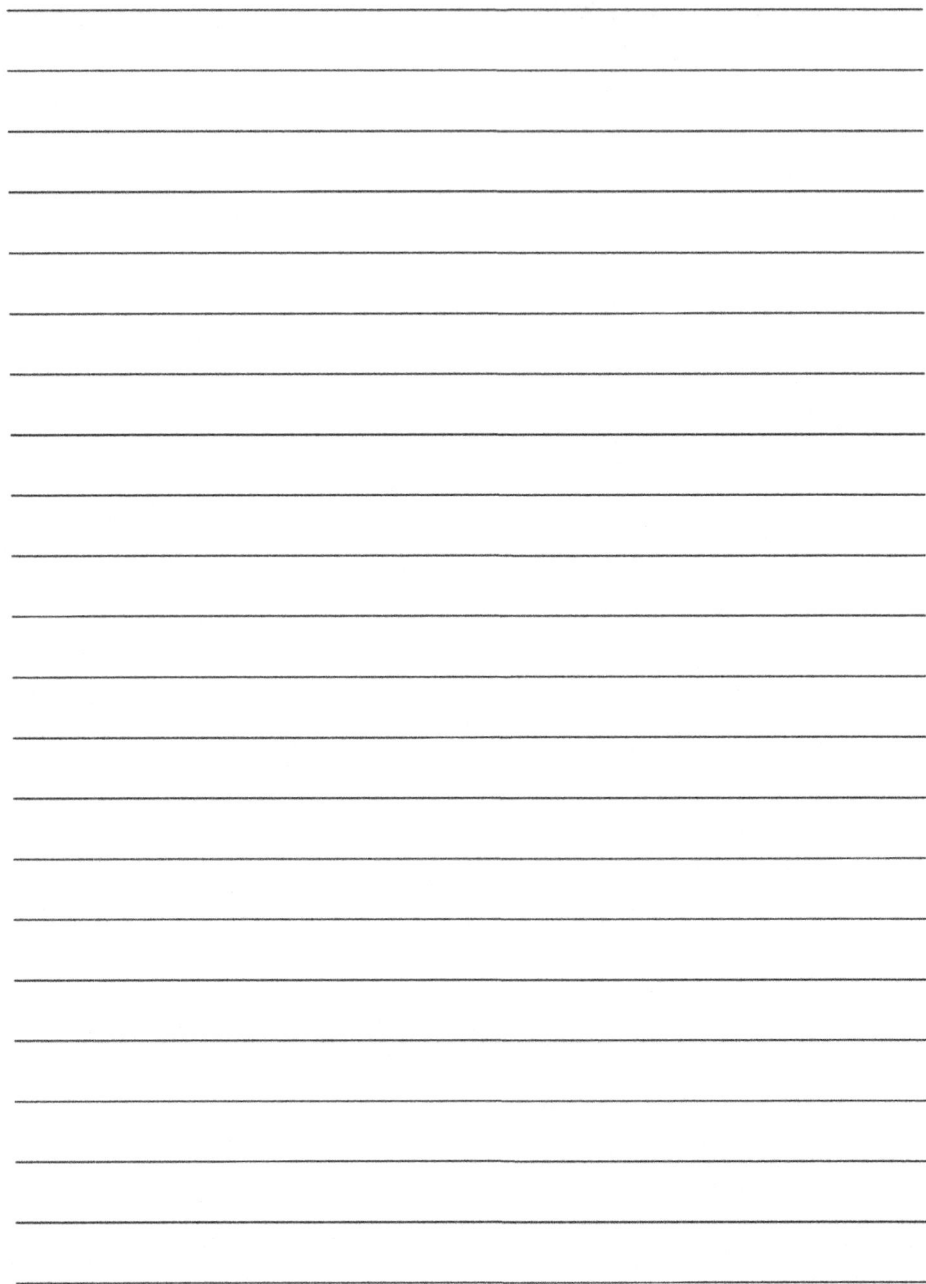

Describe your perfect day. Write it like a diary entry as if it has already happened.

DATE _____

_____

_____

_____

_____

_____

_____

_____

_____

_____

_____

_____

_____

_____

_____

_____

_____

_____

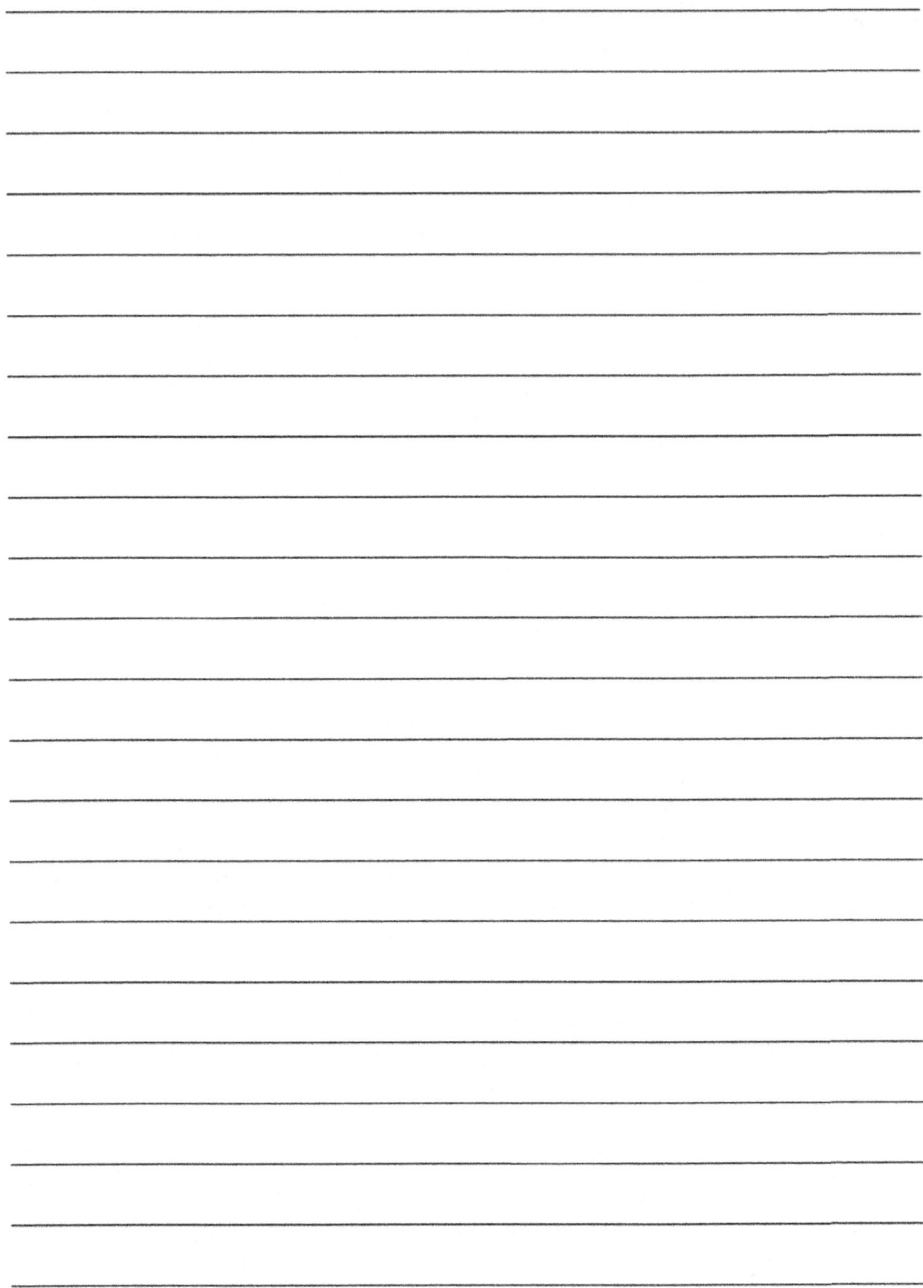

Reflect on a time when you took a
risk and it paid off.

DATE _____

_____

_____

_____

_____

_____

_____

_____

_____

_____

_____

_____

_____

_____

_____

_____

_____

_____

_____

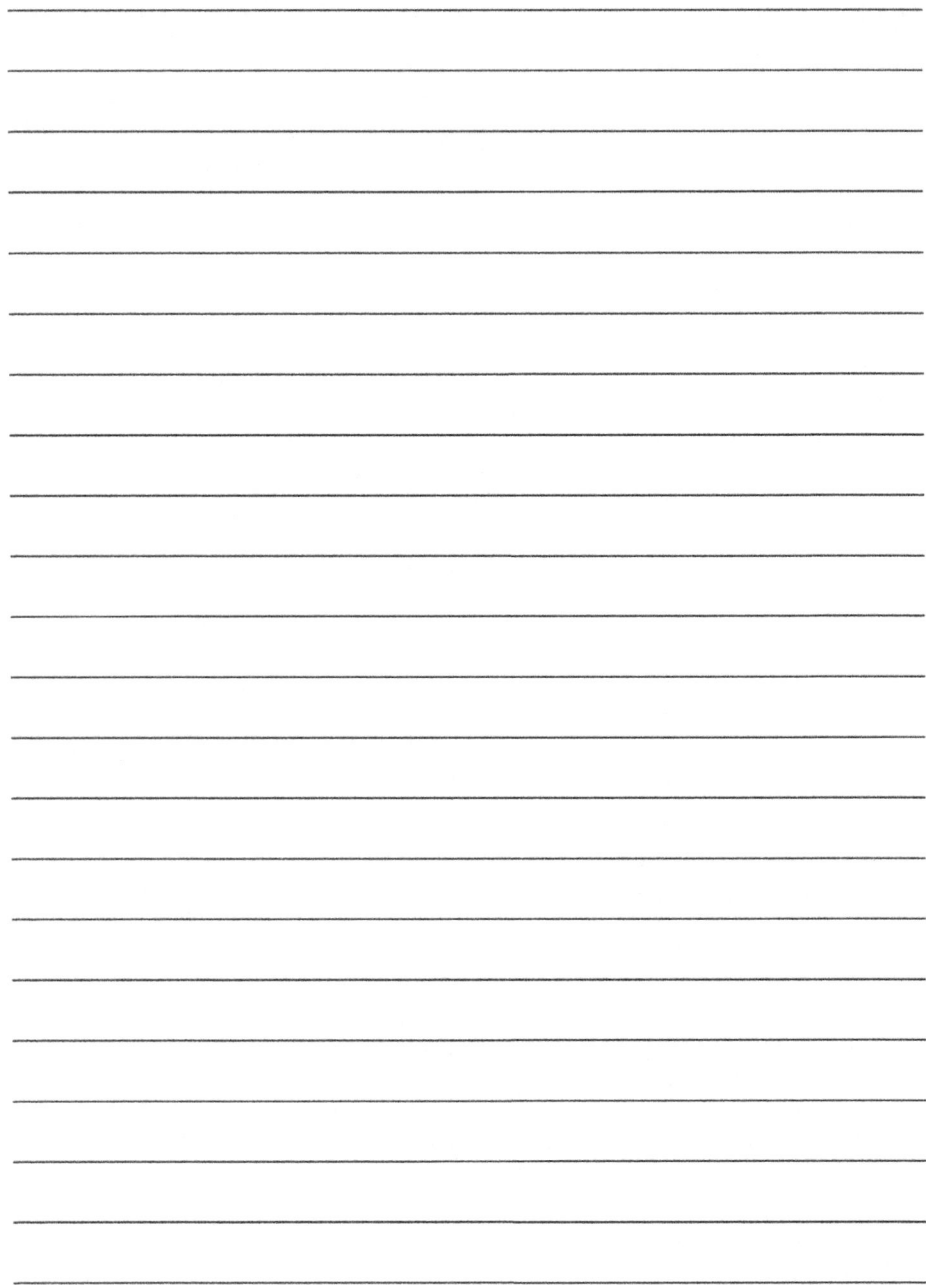

List your short-term and long-term life goals.

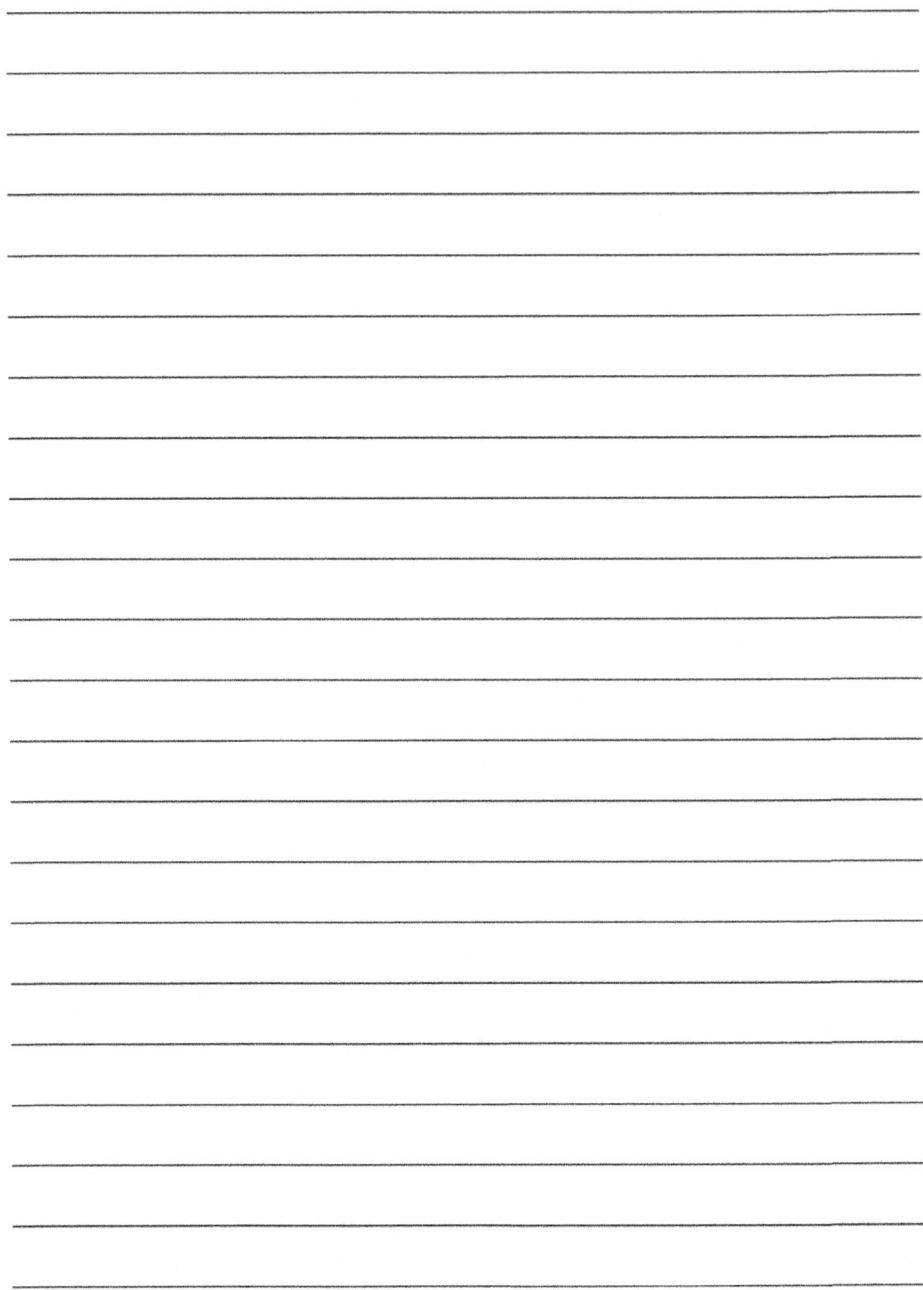

HALF FULL

Fill the cup with the things you feel positive and hopeful about, and on the next page, write the opposite. Then, ponder on your answers.

HALF EMPTY

How do you handle stress and
anxiety? What are four things you
could put in place to support stress
reduction?

DATE

_____

_____

_____

_____

_____

_____

_____

_____

_____

_____

_____

_____

_____

_____

_____

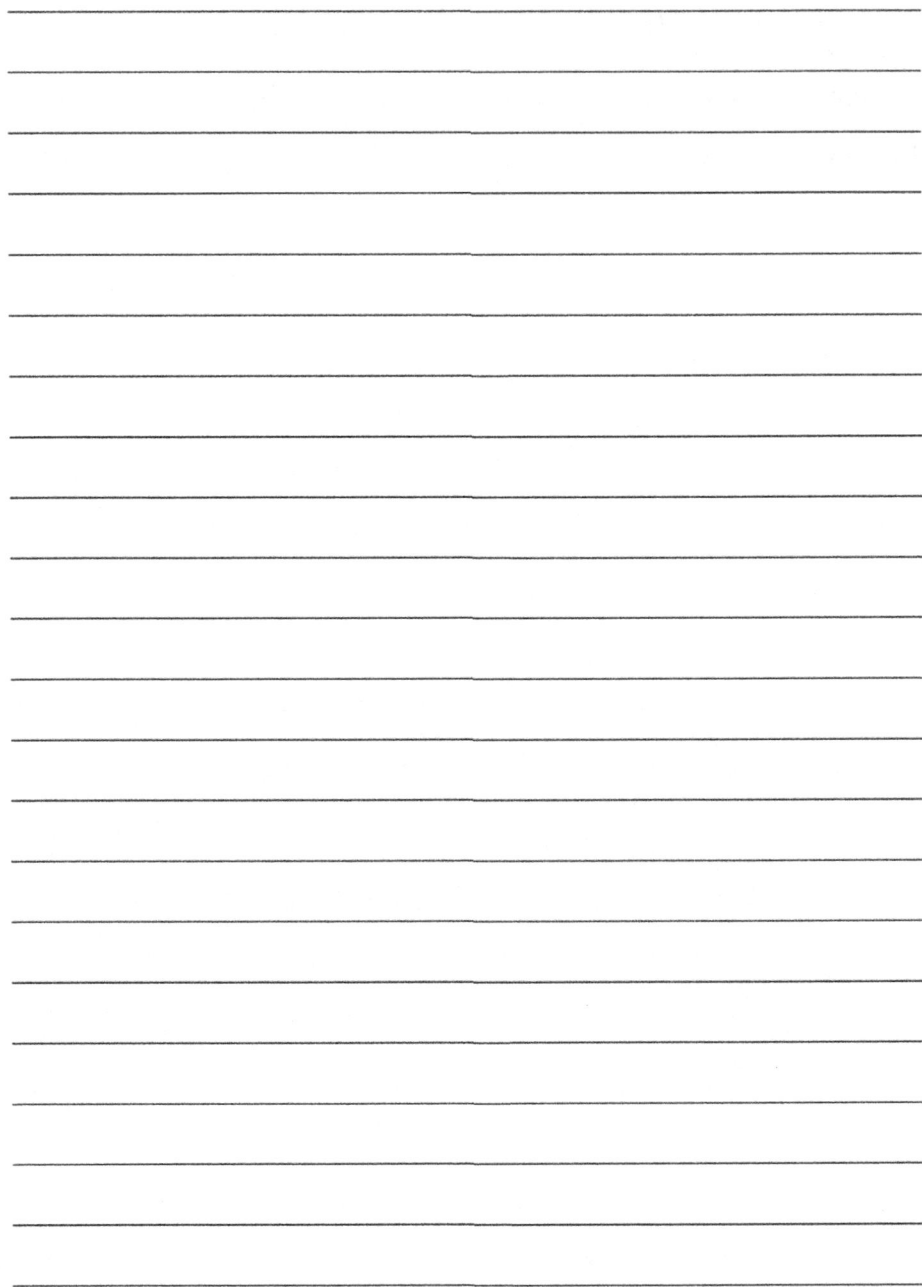

Write about a compliment that deeply touched you. Who was it from, and what was said? Why did it resonate with you on a deep level?

_____

_____

_____

_____

_____

_____

_____

_____

_____

_____

_____

_____

_____

_____

_____

_____

_____

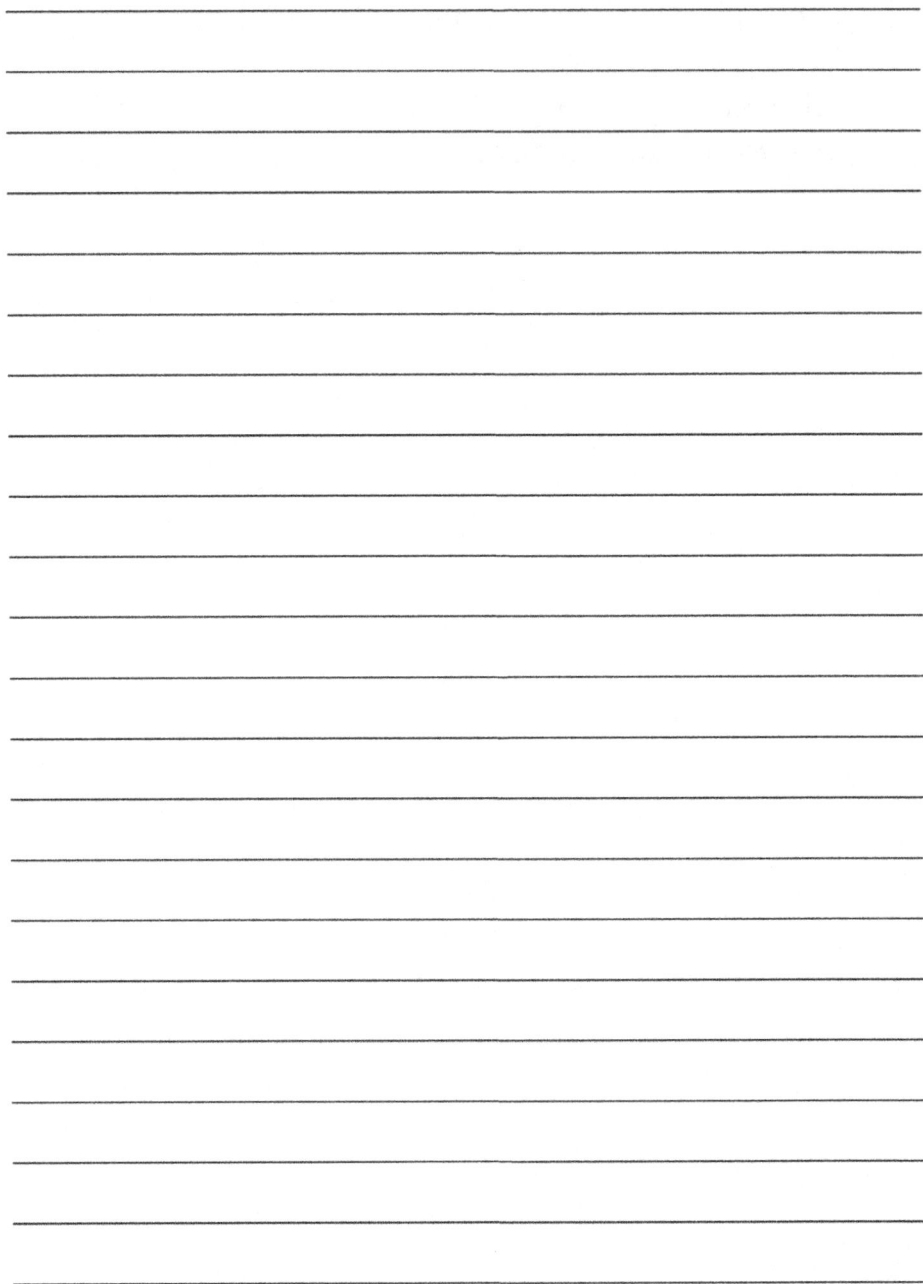

How do you forgive yourself for past mistakes? Delve into four ideas or strategies that could aid in self-compassion.

_____

_____

_____

_____

_____

_____

_____

_____

_____

_____

_____

_____

_____

_____

_____

_____

_____

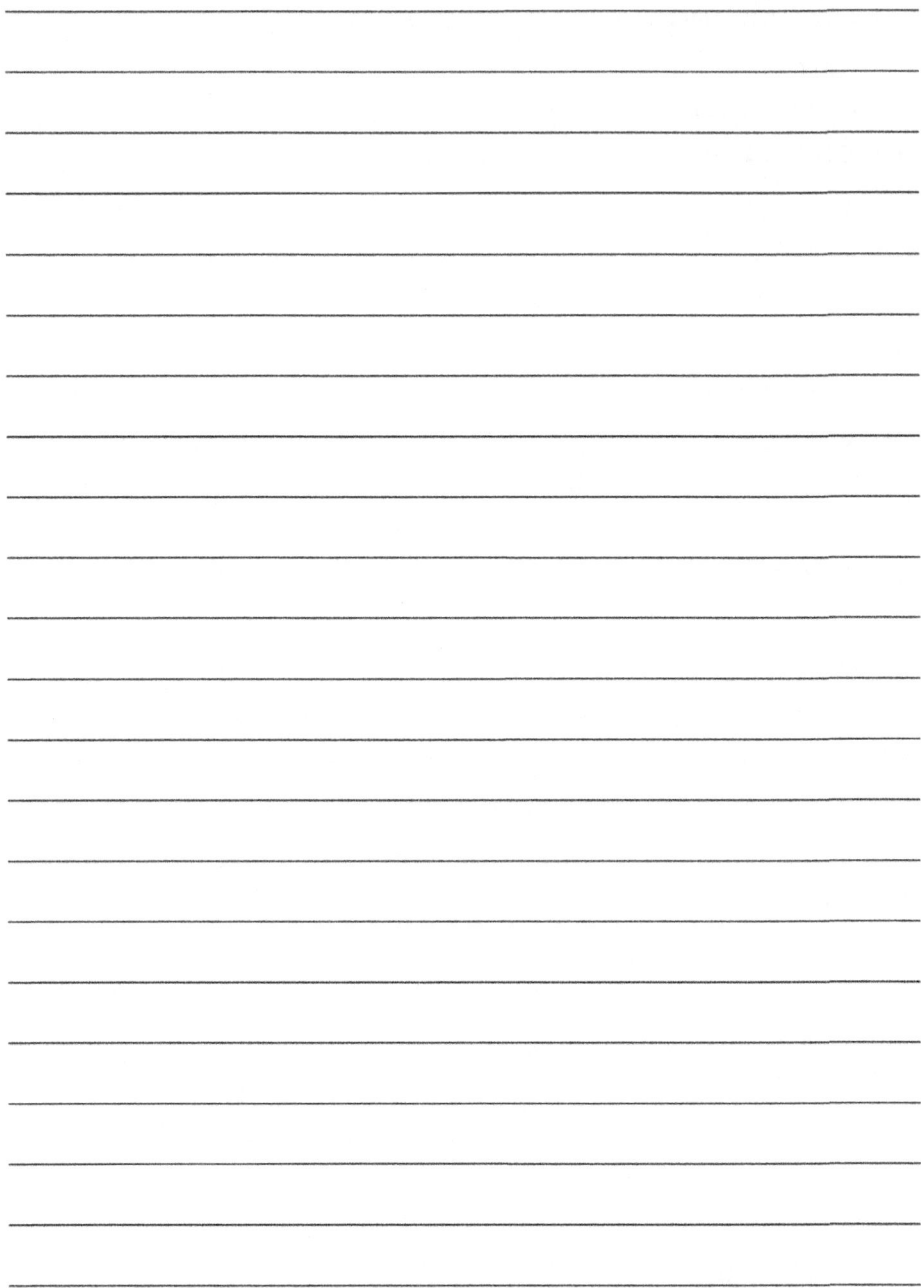

What is your vision for a fulfilling life?

DATE _____

_____

_____

_____

_____

_____

_____

_____

_____

_____

_____

_____

_____

_____

_____

_____

_____

_____

_____

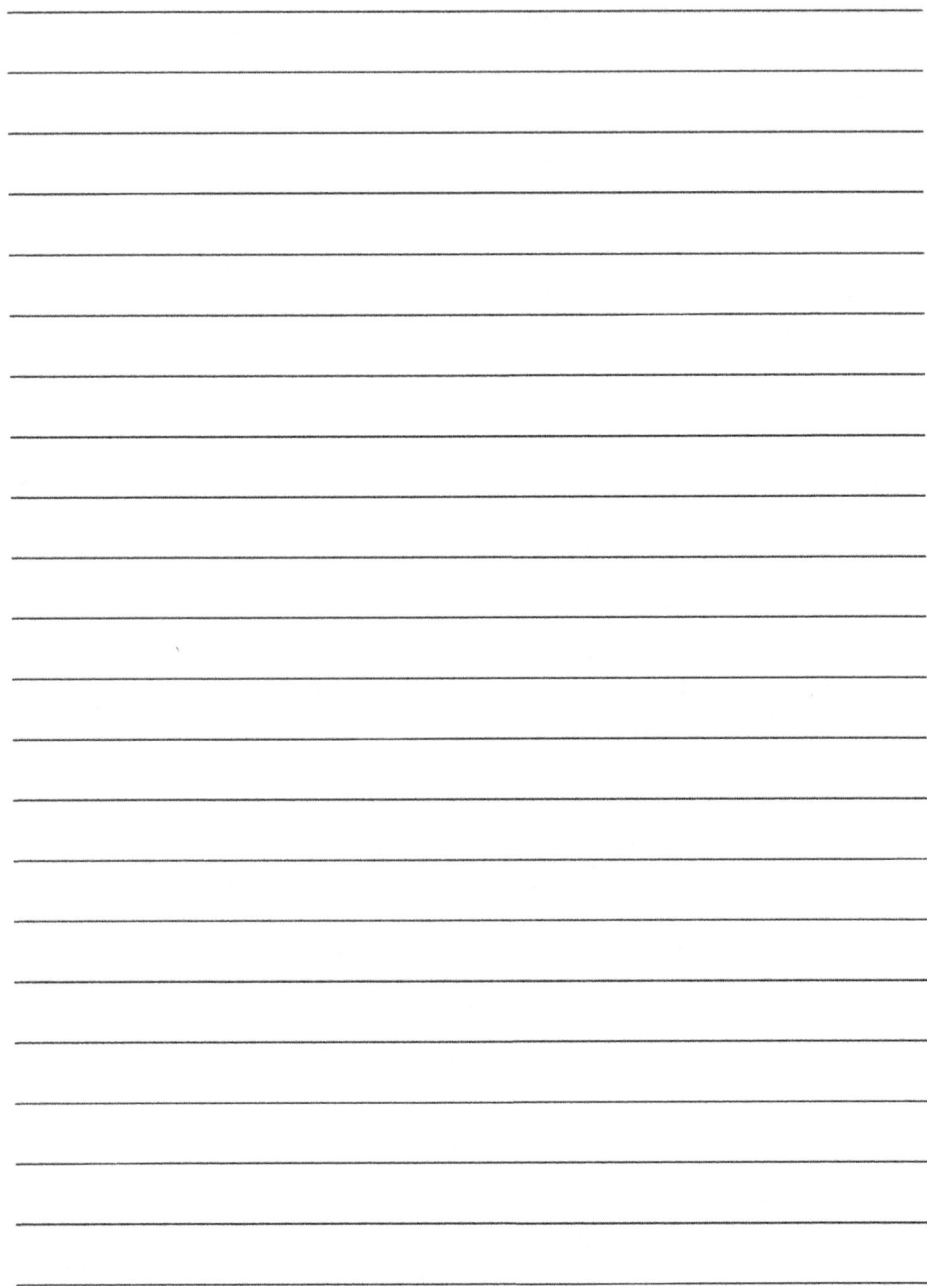

Describe a place where you feel truly content and at ease. Describe why it's important to feel this way.

_____

_____

_____

_____

_____

_____

_____

_____

_____

_____

_____

_____

_____

_____

_____

_____

_____

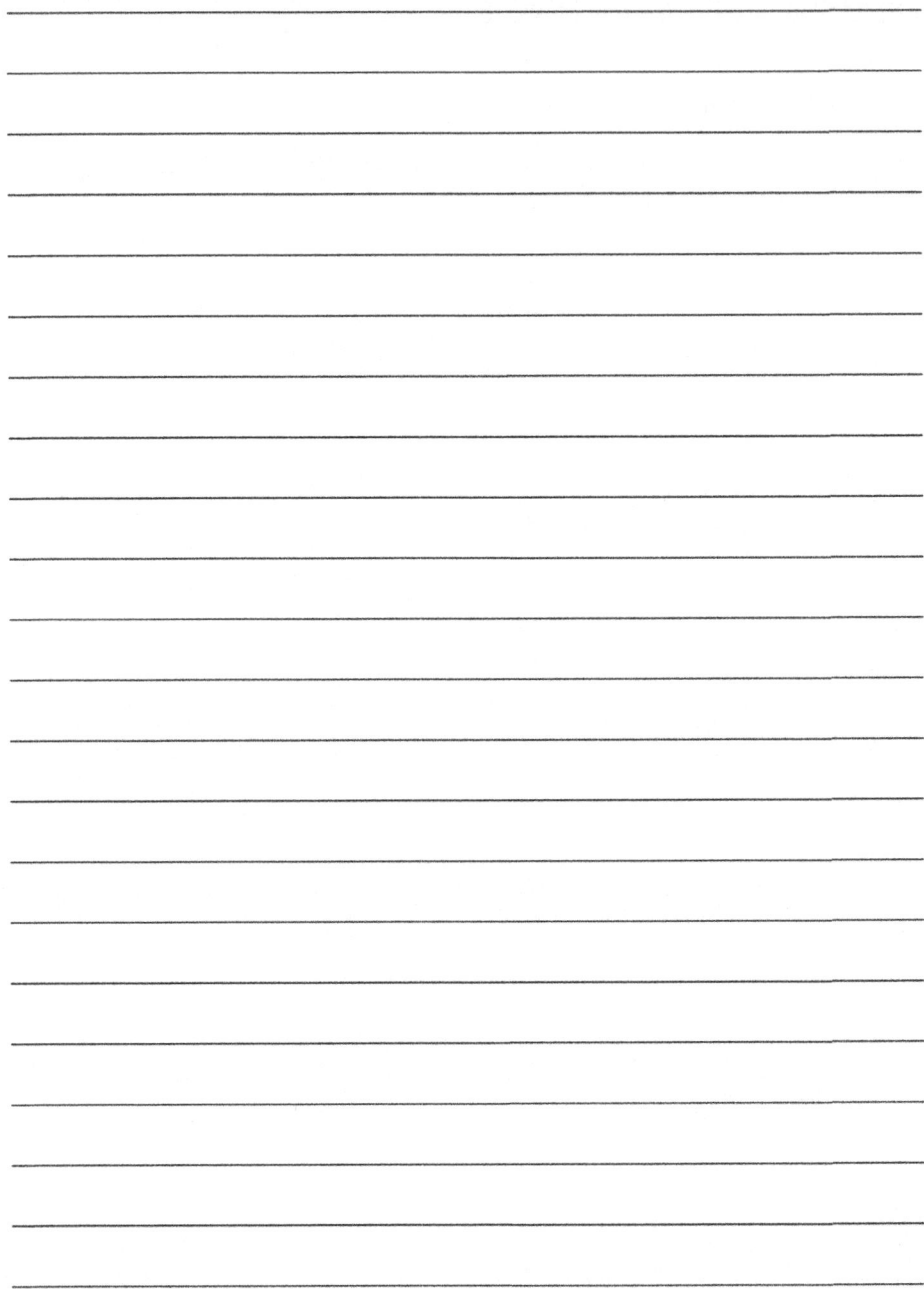

My Ultimate Coping Playlist

Music can be therapeutic. Make a list of songs that you know will uplift your mood.

FOR FUN

----

a song that gets stuck in my head

----

a song I know all the words to

----

a song from my favorite movie or tv series

TO UPLIFT ME

----

a song I associate with freedom

----

a song that gives me energy

----

a song I'd like to wake me up

FOR MOTIVATION

----
a song that makes
me feel safe

----
a song that helps me
think positively

----
a song that inspires
me

TO DE-STRESS

----
a song that helps me
feel calm

----
a song that reminds
me of the beauty of life

----
a song that reminds
me of the beauty of
nature

FOR MEMORIES

----
a song that reminds
me of a good memory

----
a song that makes me
think of a loved one

----
a song to remind me
that I am important

How can you be more present and
mindful in your daily life? What are
some ways to get started?

DATE _____

_____

_____

_____

_____

_____

_____

_____

_____

_____

_____

_____

_____

_____

_____

_____

_____

_____

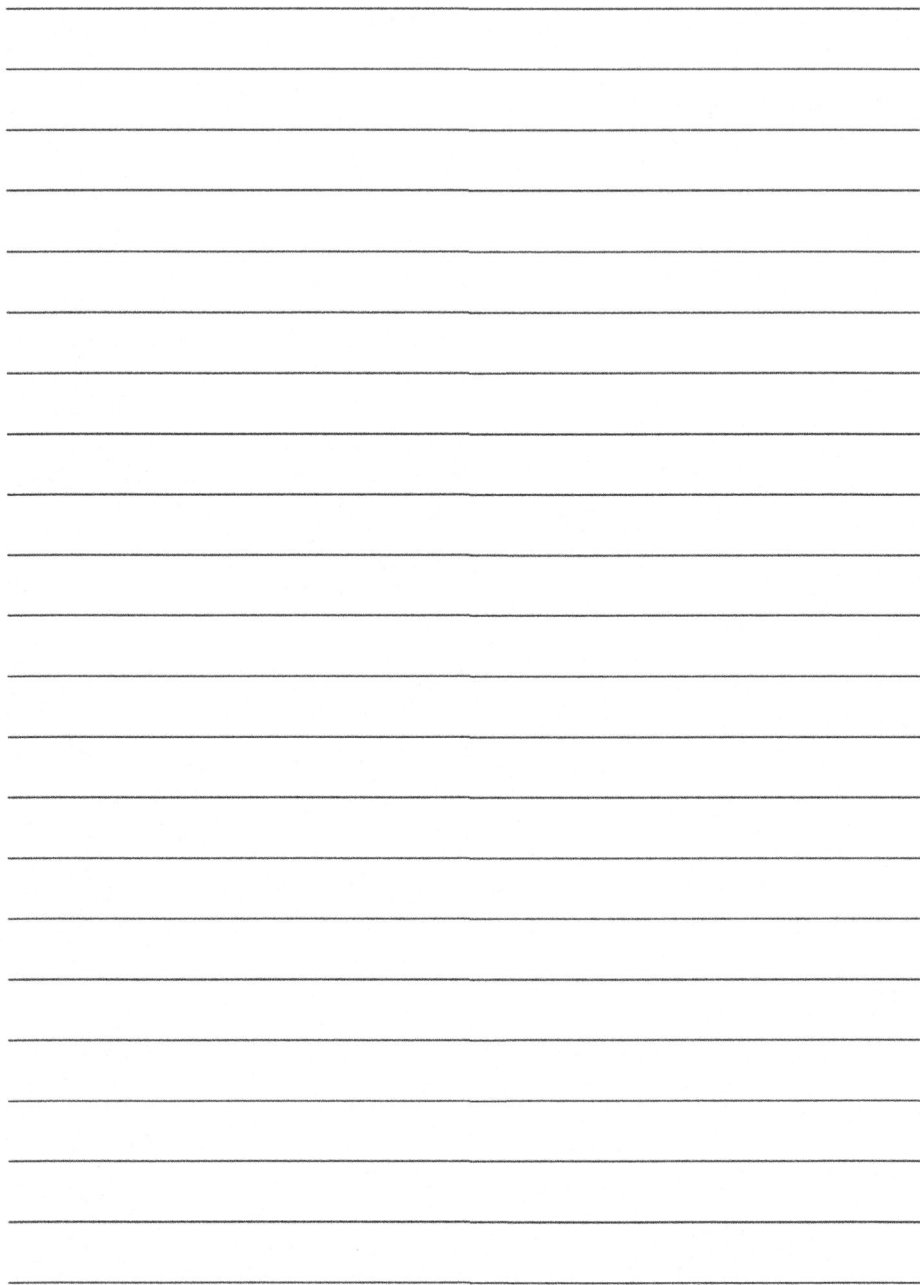

Write a letter of gratitude to your body. Reflect on how you can commit to treating your body with more kindness, respect, and care.

DATE _____

_____

_____

_____

_____

_____

_____

_____

_____

_____

_____

_____

_____

_____

_____

_____

_____

_____

_____

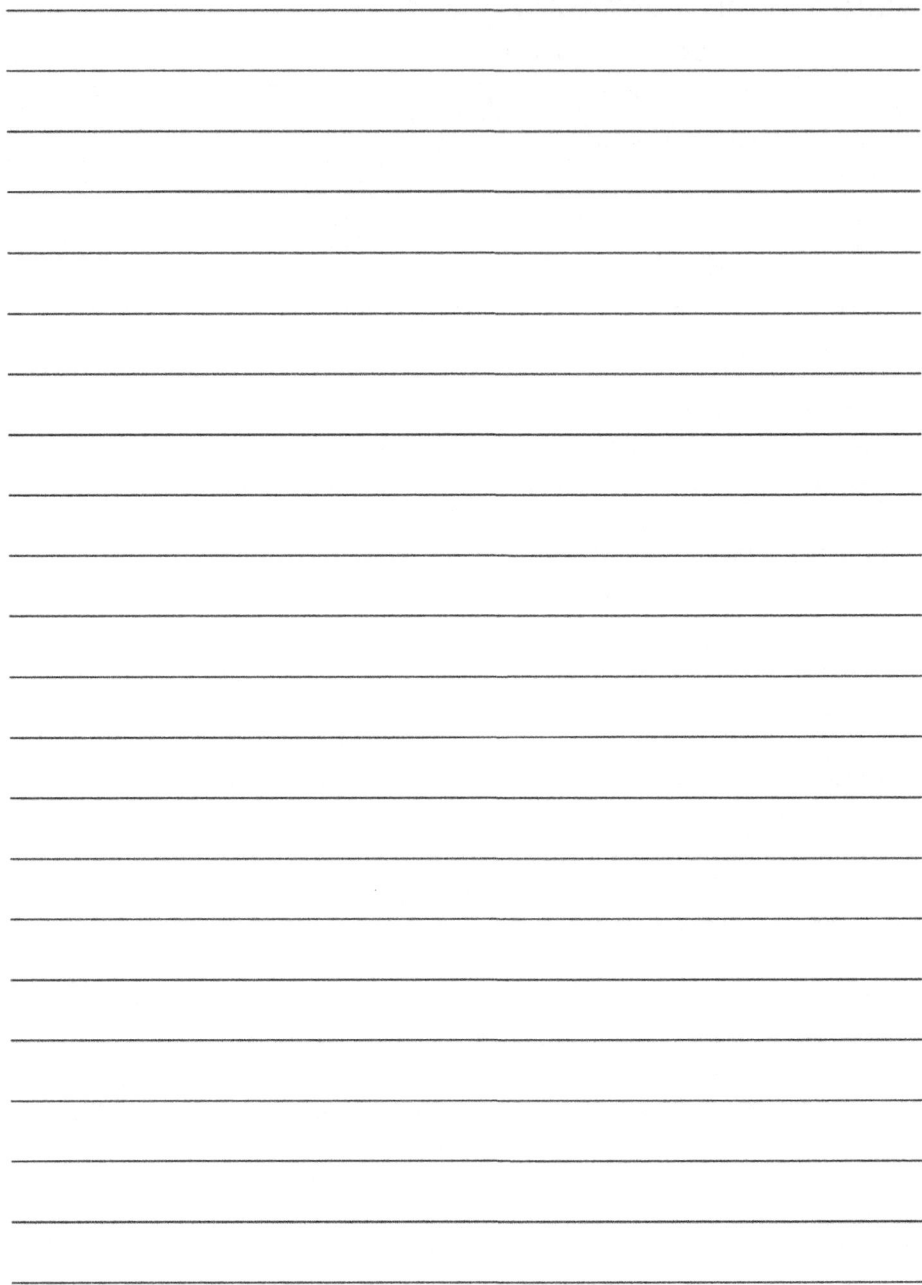

What are your favorite affirmations for self-love? If you don't have any, write seven, one for each day of the week.

DATE _____

_____

_____

_____

_____

_____

_____

_____

_____

_____

_____

_____

_____

_____

_____

_____

_____

_____

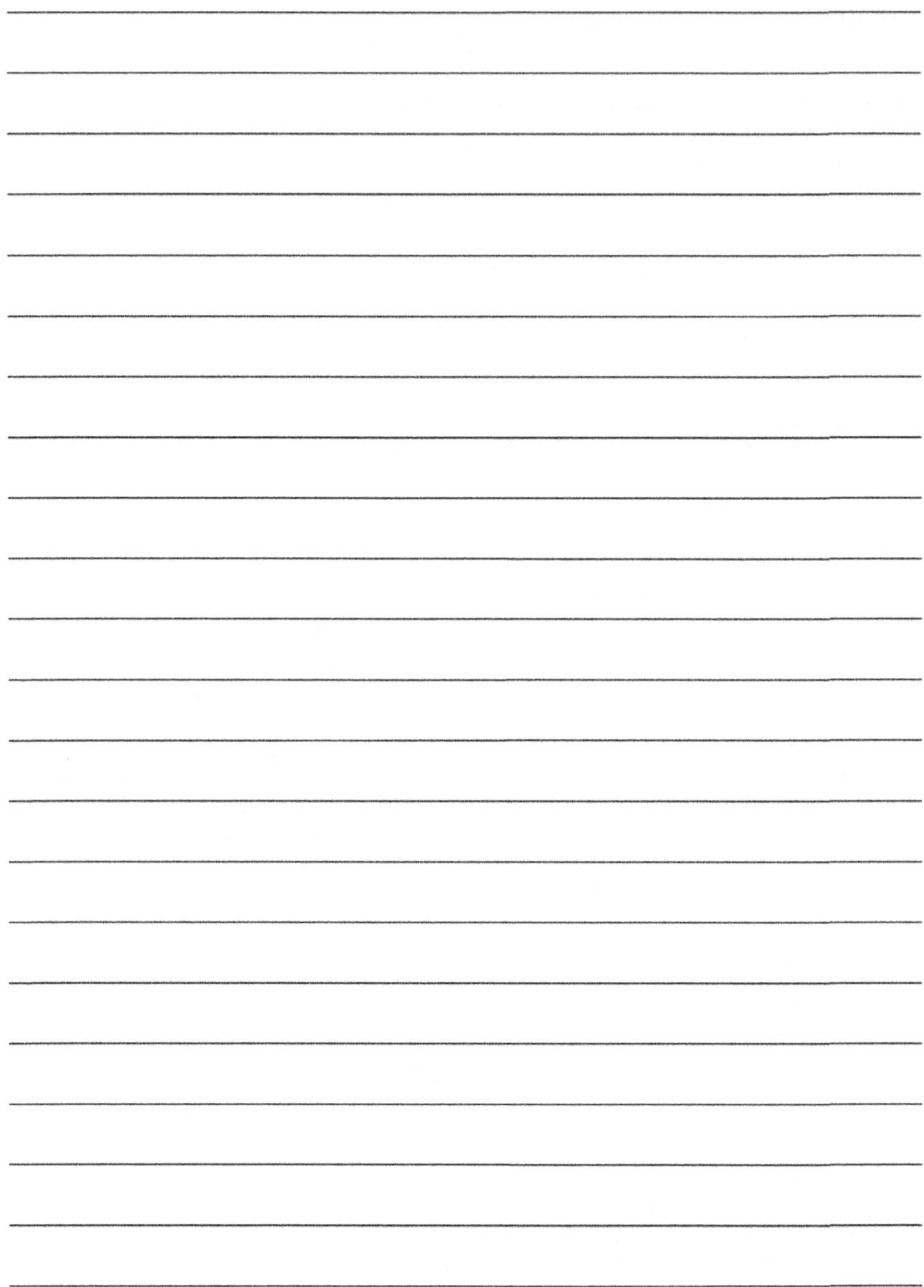

How do you define success? How has your definition evolved over time? What factors have influenced this evolution?

_____

_____

_____

_____

_____

_____

_____

_____

_____

_____

_____

_____

_____

_____

_____

_____

_____

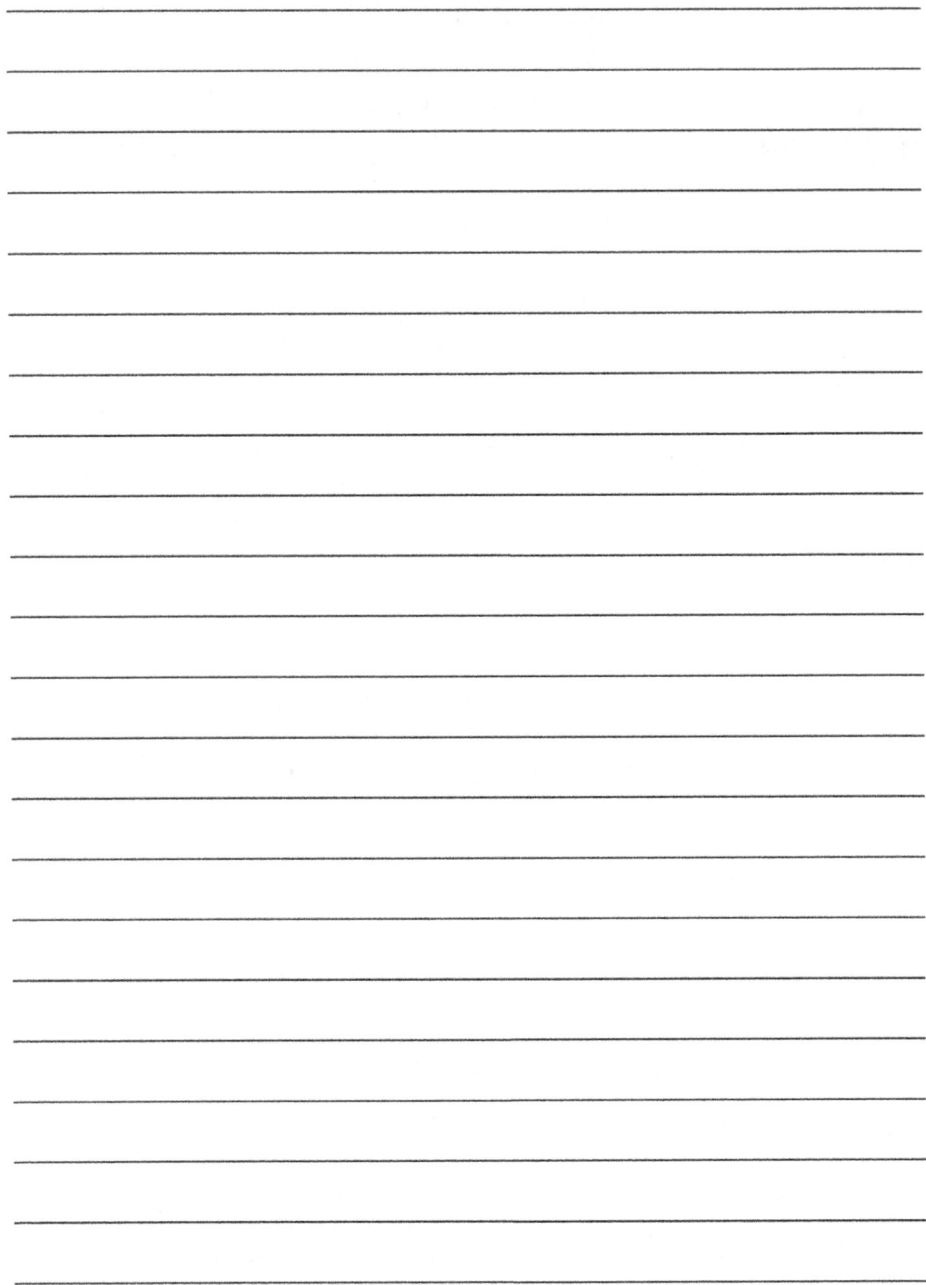

List four things that always make
you smile and why they do. How
can you incorporate them into your
regular routine?

DATE _____

_____

_____

_____

_____

_____

_____

_____

_____

_____

_____

_____

_____

_____

_____

_____

_____

_____

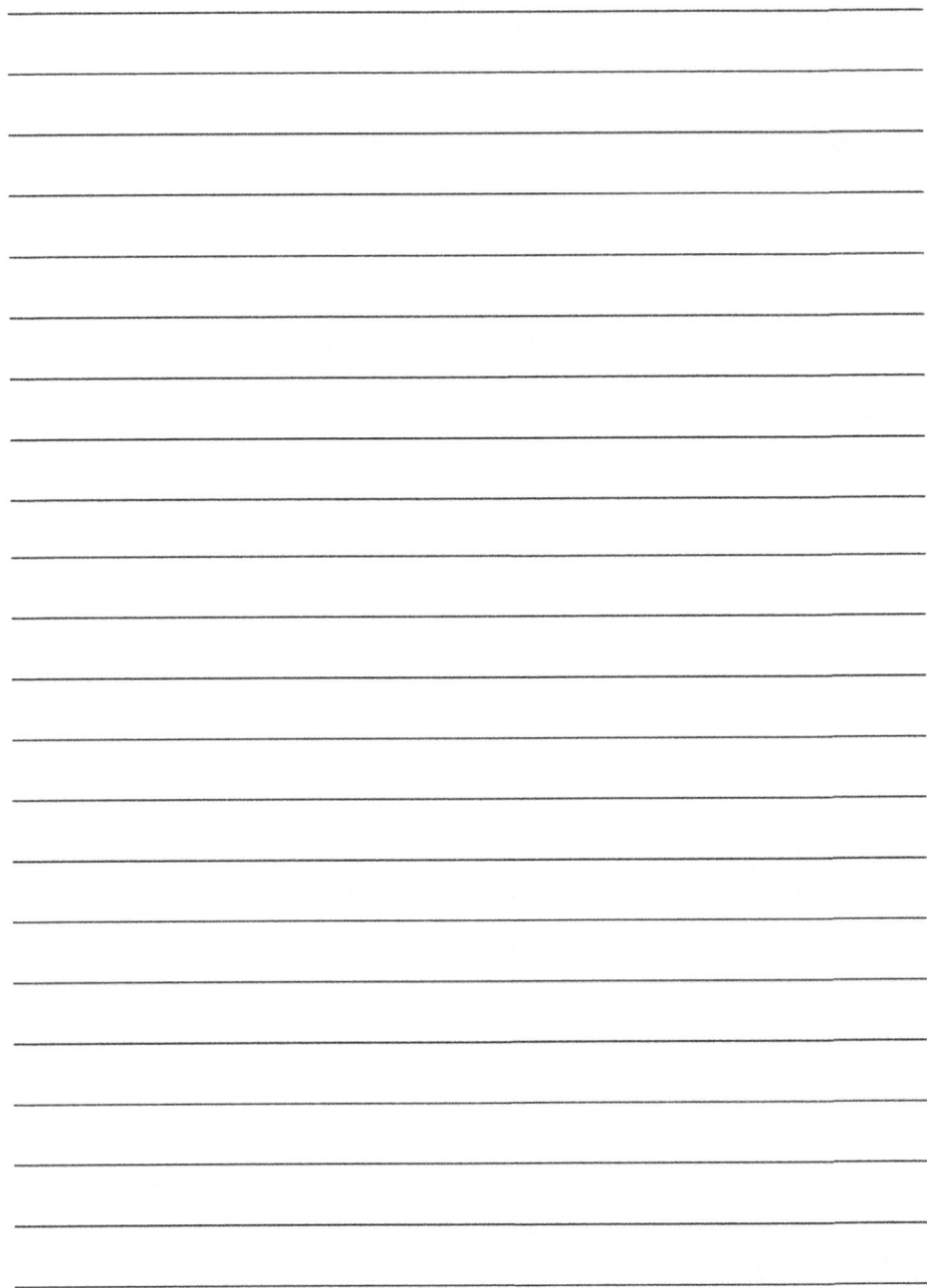

THE RELEASE

Use this space to write things you need to let go of
on the left and action items on the right that will
help you practice the release.

Heart-Centered

Trace the letters

I am loved

I am important

I am unique

I am growing

I forgive

I embrace joy

I am love

Reflect on a time when you showed yourself kindness. How did it make you feel? Describe the circumstances.

_____

_____

_____

_____

_____

_____

_____

_____

_____

_____

_____

_____

_____

_____

_____

_____

_____

_____

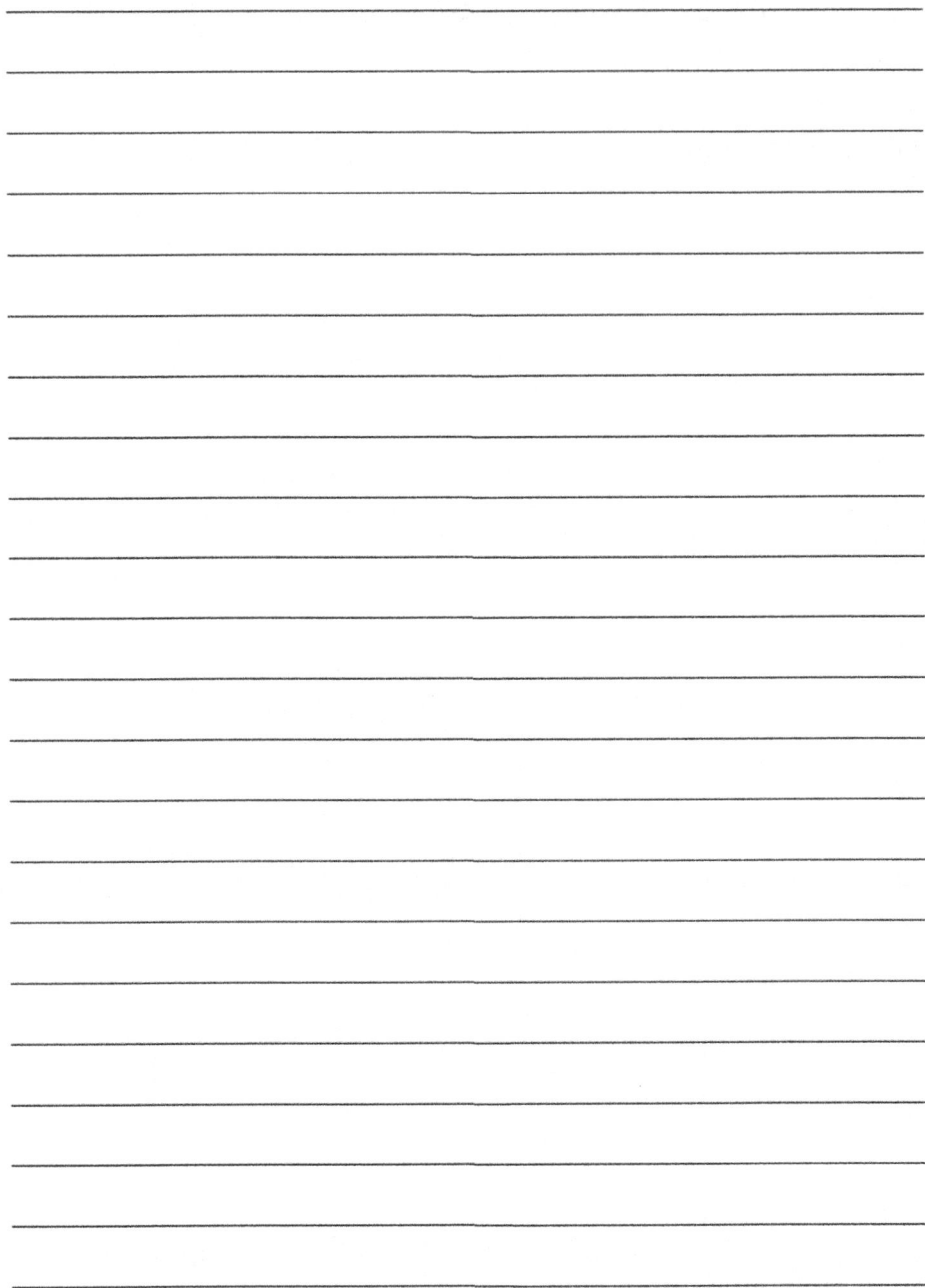

How important are boundaries to
you? How can you set healthy
boundaries in your relationships?

DATE _____

_____

_____

_____

_____

_____

_____

_____

_____

_____

_____

_____

_____

_____

_____

_____

_____

_____

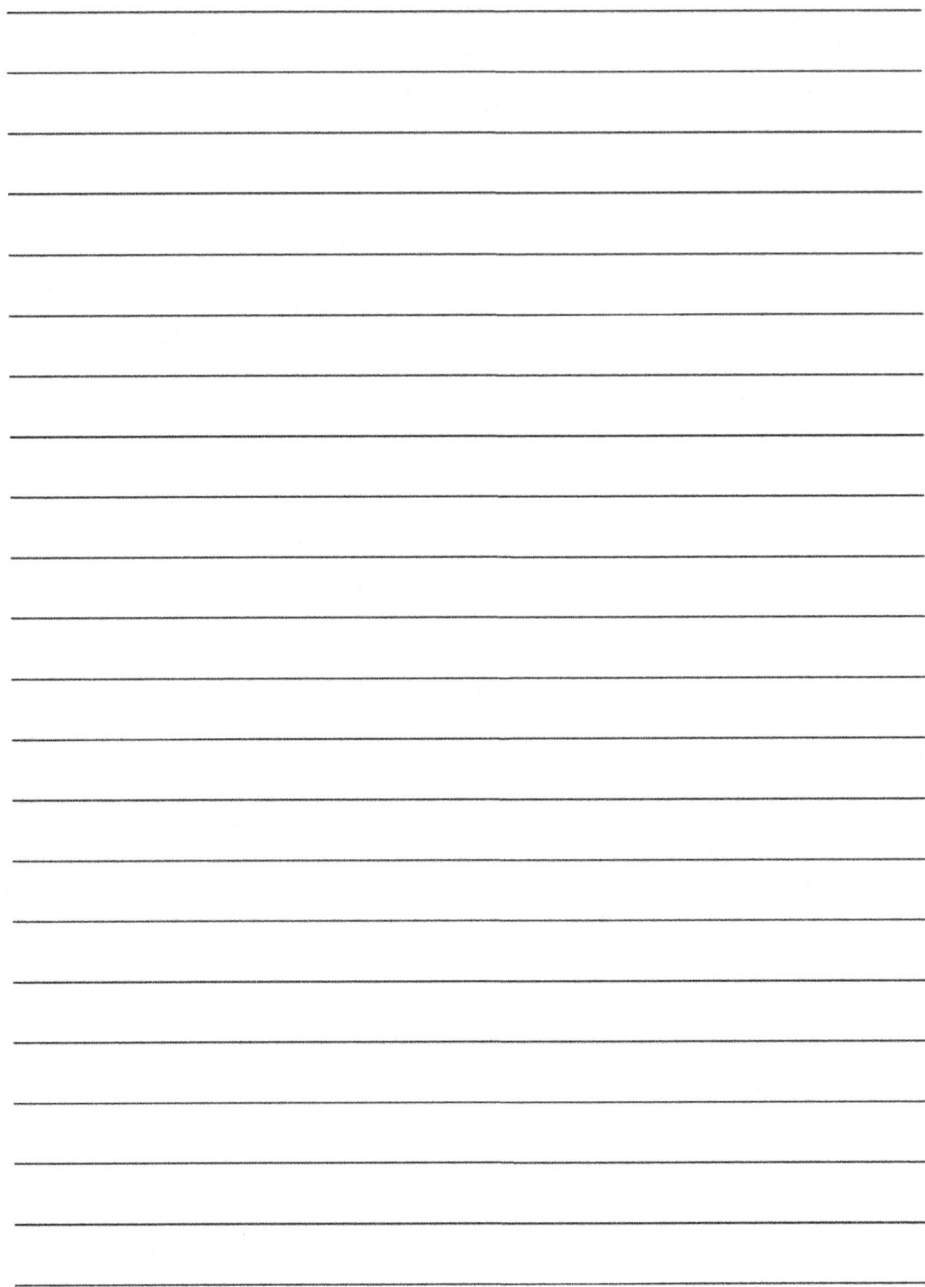

Reflect on the activities that drain your energy. How can you reduce or re-arrange those activities to lighten your load?

_____

_____

_____

_____

_____

_____

_____

_____

_____

_____

_____

_____

_____

_____

_____

_____

_____

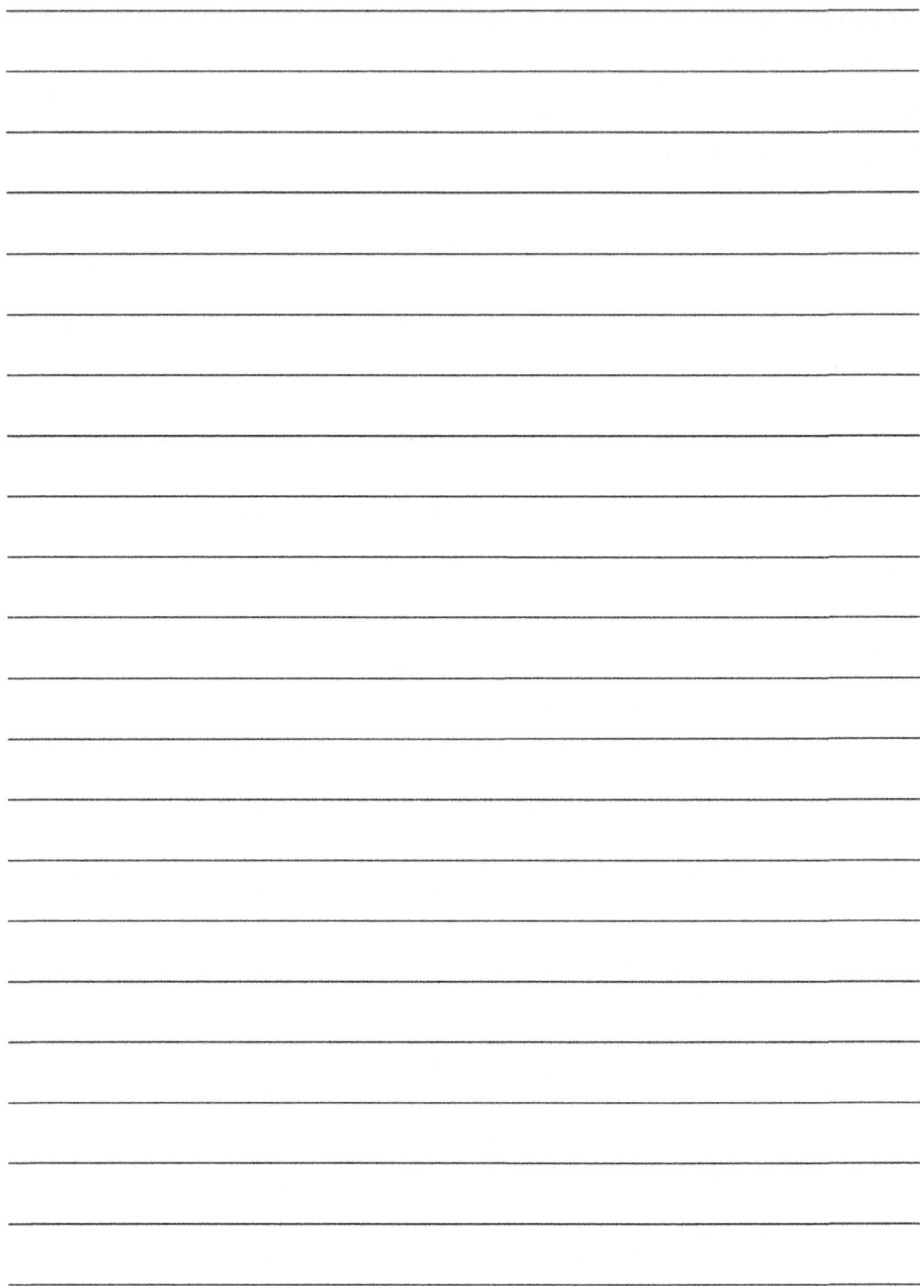

List a few people who inspire you
and describe why.

_____

_____

_____

_____

_____

_____

_____

_____

_____

_____

_____

_____

_____

_____

_____

_____

_____

_____

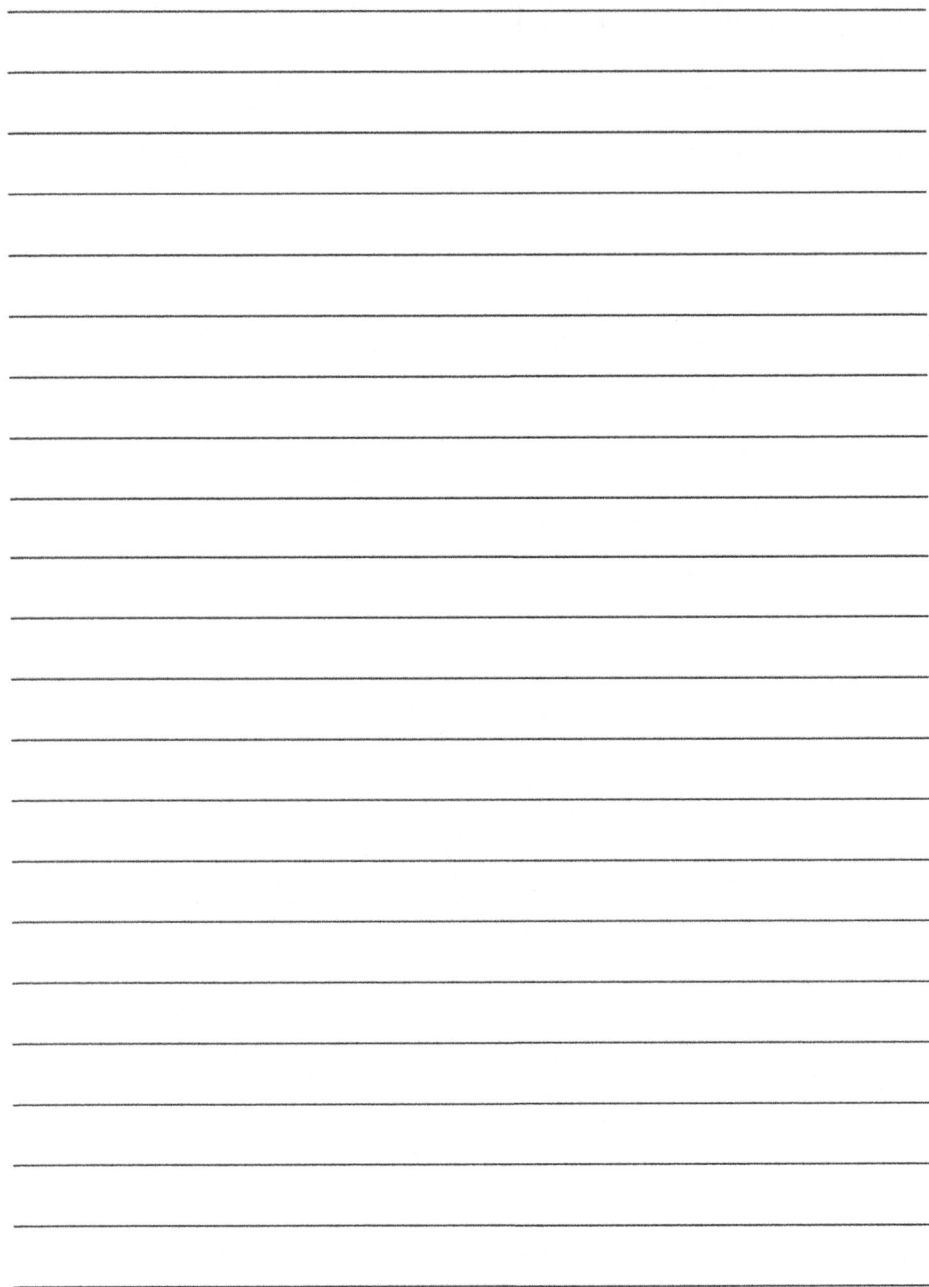

Do you have someone in your life
you consider an accountability
partner? What are important
qualities for this person to have?

DATE _____

_____

_____

_____

_____

_____

_____

_____

_____

_____

_____

_____

_____

_____

_____

_____

_____

_____

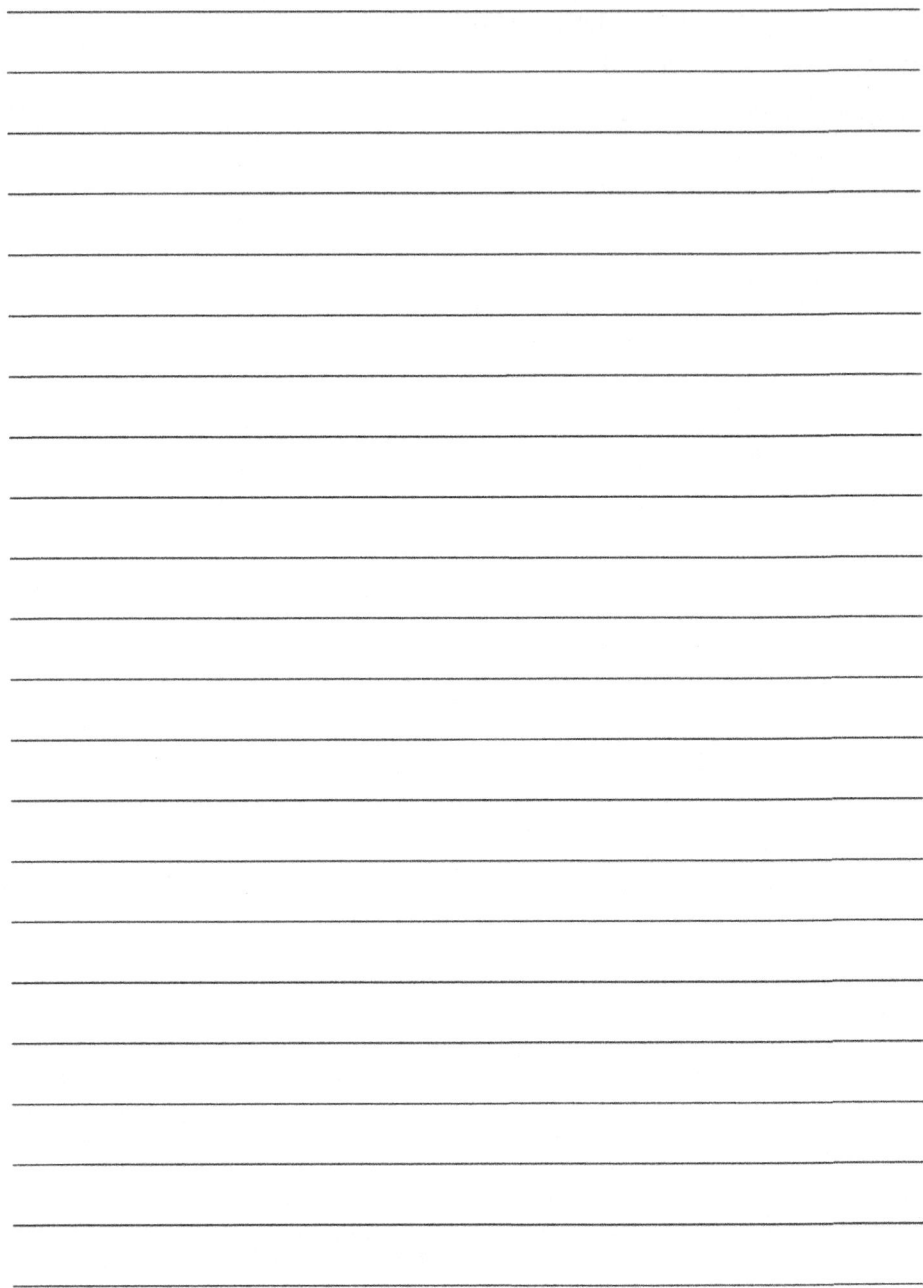

Self-reflection is empowerment.

COLOR
THE FLOWERS

Reflect on your approach to
handling setbacks and failures in
life. How has it evolved over time?   DATE _____
What have you learned?

_____

_____

_____

_____

_____

_____

_____

_____

_____

_____

_____

_____

_____

_____

_____

_____

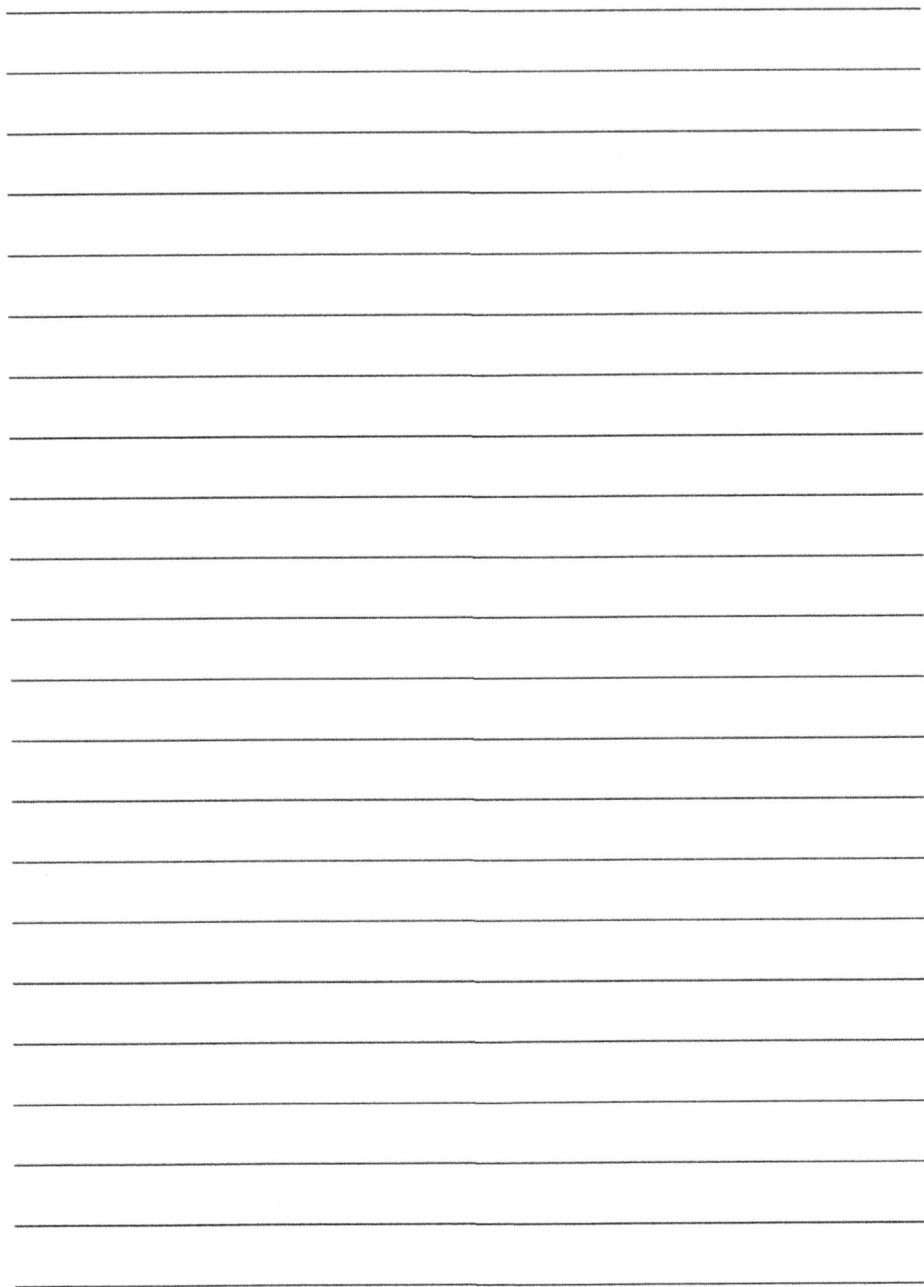

List the books that have inspired
your self-love journey and why.
Also, list any that you want to read.

DATE _____

_____

_____

_____

_____

_____

_____

_____

_____

_____

_____

_____

_____

_____

_____

_____

_____

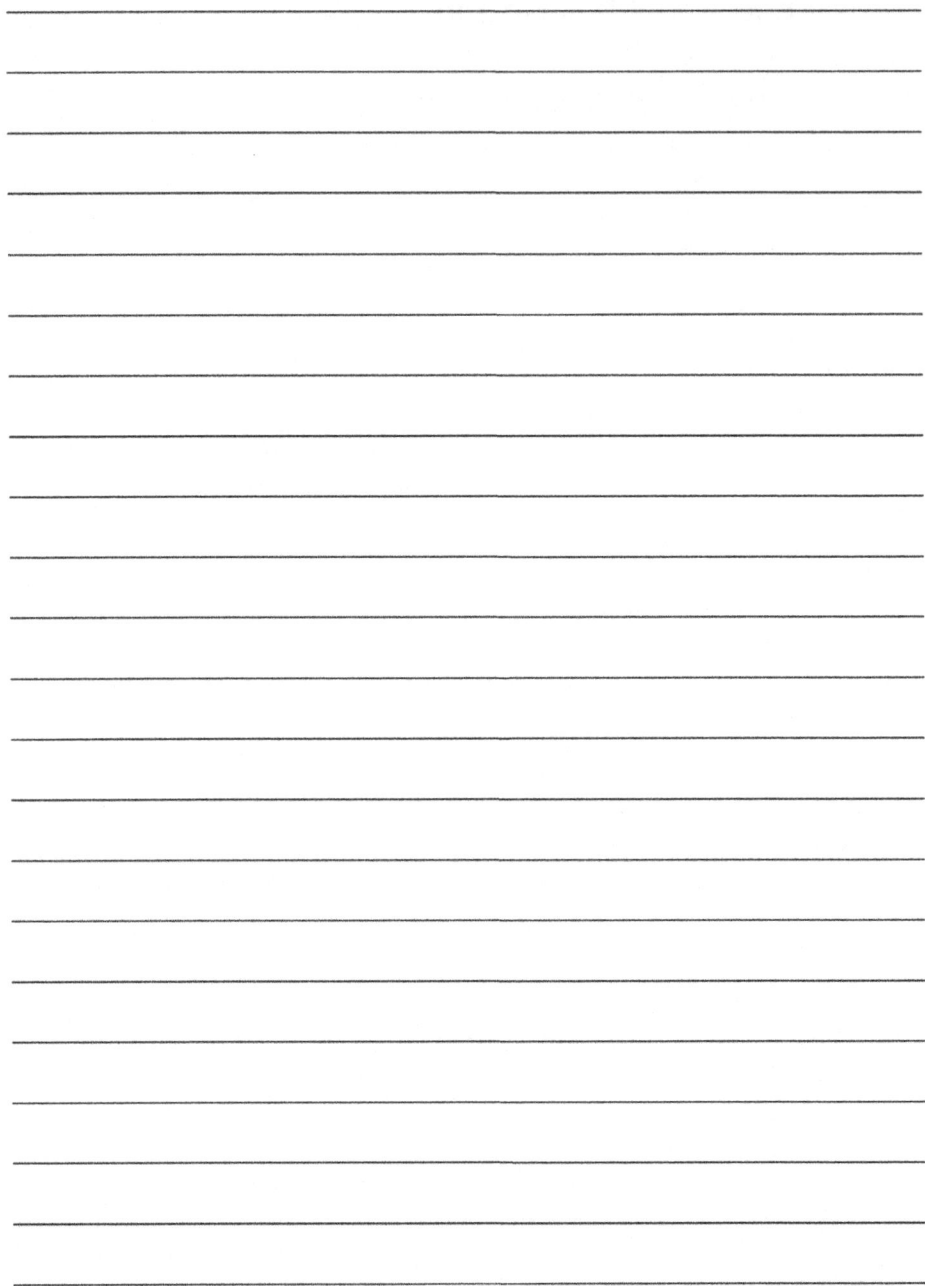

What does spirituality mean to you?
Is it an important part of your life? If
so, list the reasons why.

DATE _____

_____

_____

_____

_____

_____

_____

_____

_____

_____

_____

_____

_____

_____

_____

_____

_____

_____

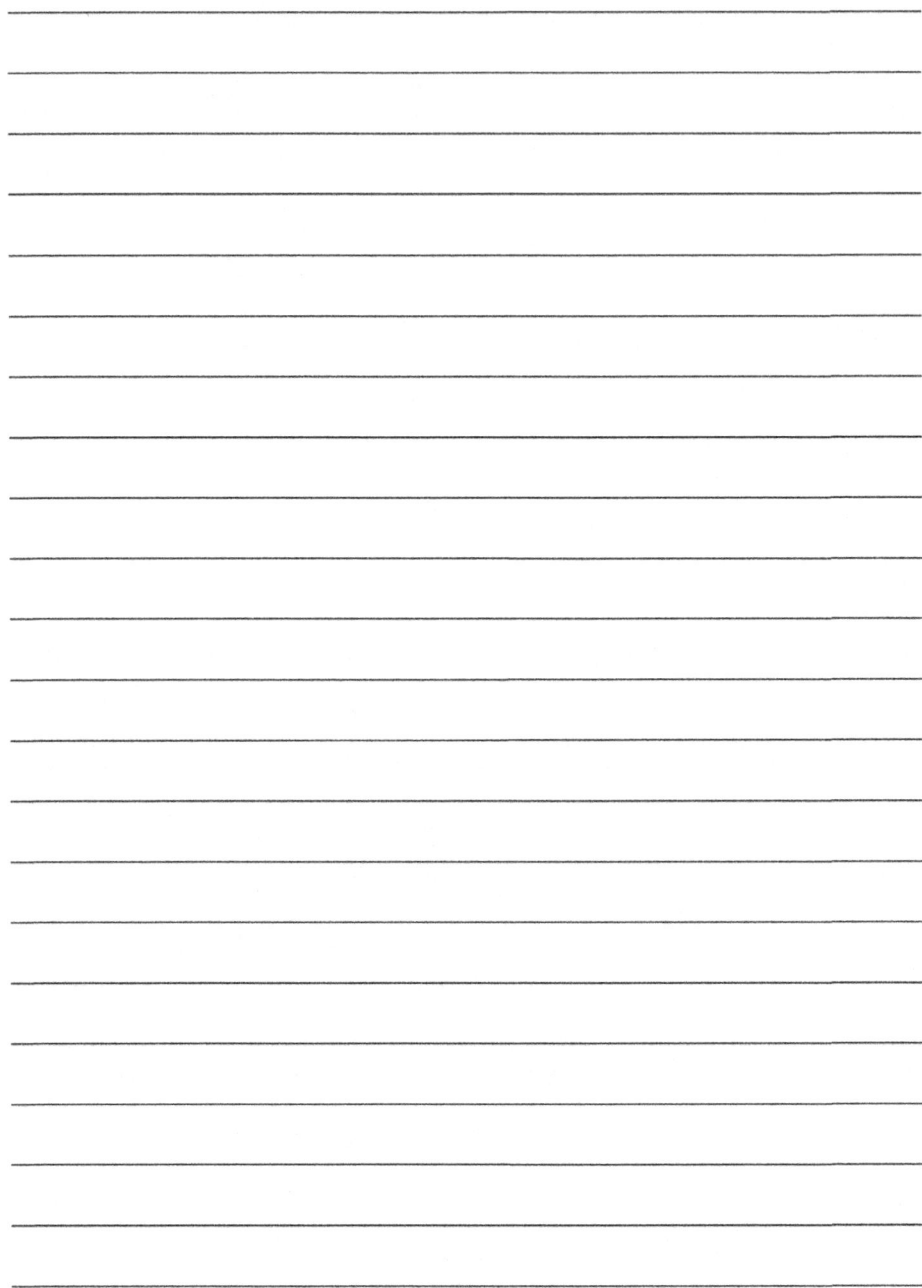

List a few fun, creative hobbies that you would like. Reflect on why you would enjoy them. Choose one to try, then pick a start date.

_____

_____

_____

_____

_____

_____

_____

_____

_____

_____

_____

_____

_____

_____

_____

_____

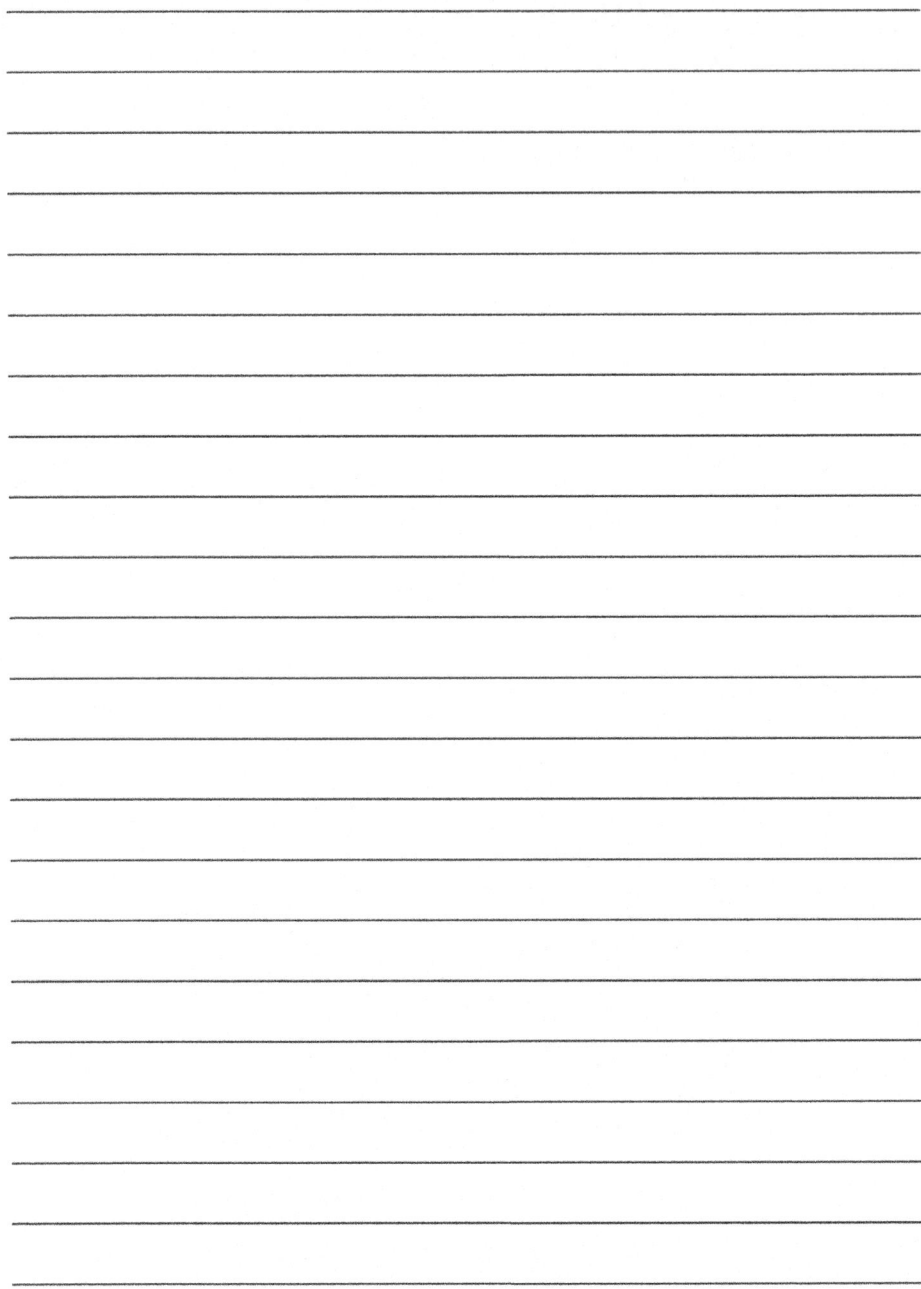

Are there any emotional needs you felt were unmet during your childhood? What healing practices can provide the comfort or support you missed?

_____

_____

_____

_____

_____

_____

_____

_____

_____

_____

_____

_____

_____

_____

_____

_____

_____

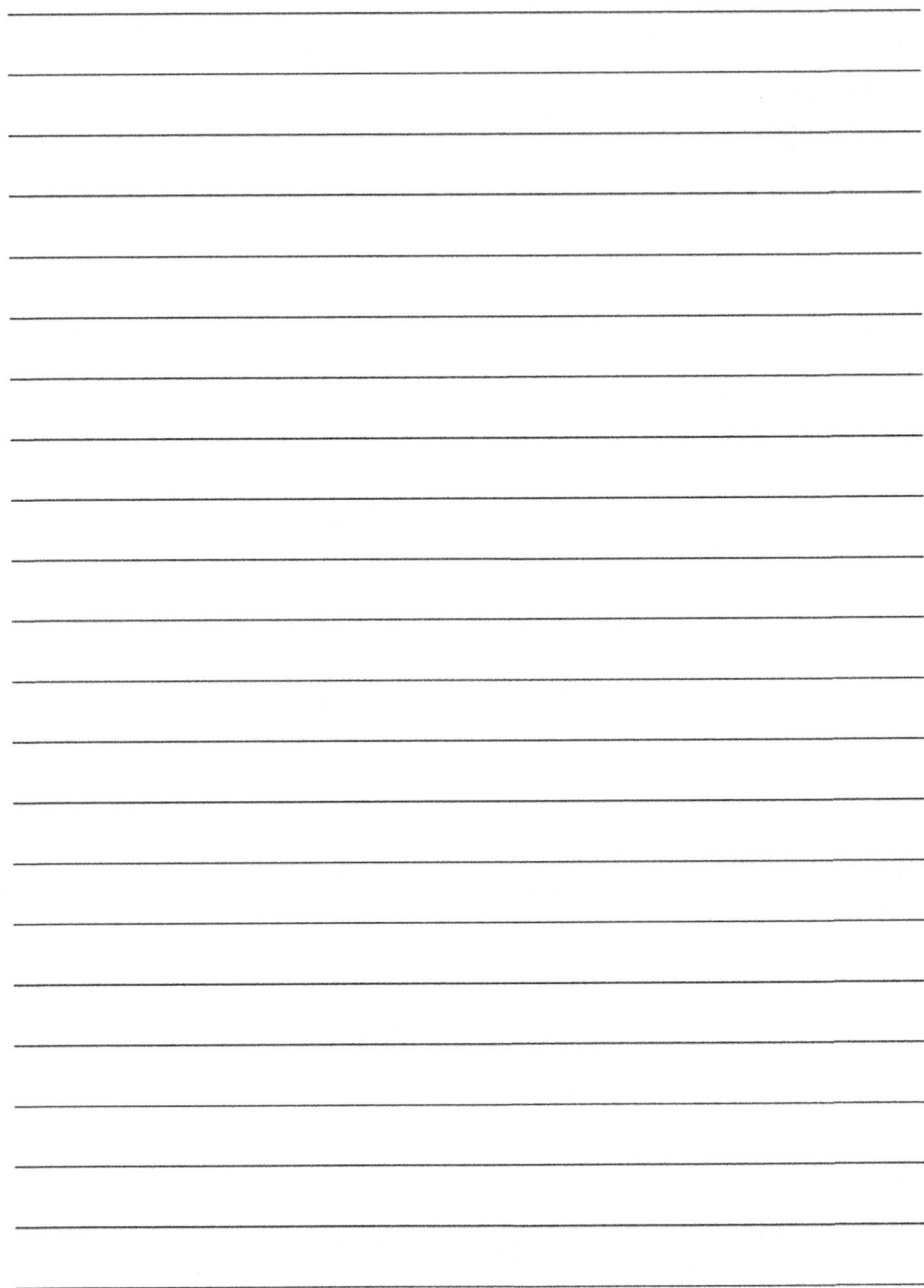

THE ENERGY BANK

THINGS THAT ADD TO MY ENERGY

THINGS THAT DEPLETE MY ENERGY

How have your friendships evolved
over the years? What attributes are
important in a good friend?   DATE _____

_____

_____

_____

_____

_____

_____

_____

_____

_____

_____

_____

_____

_____

_____

_____

_____

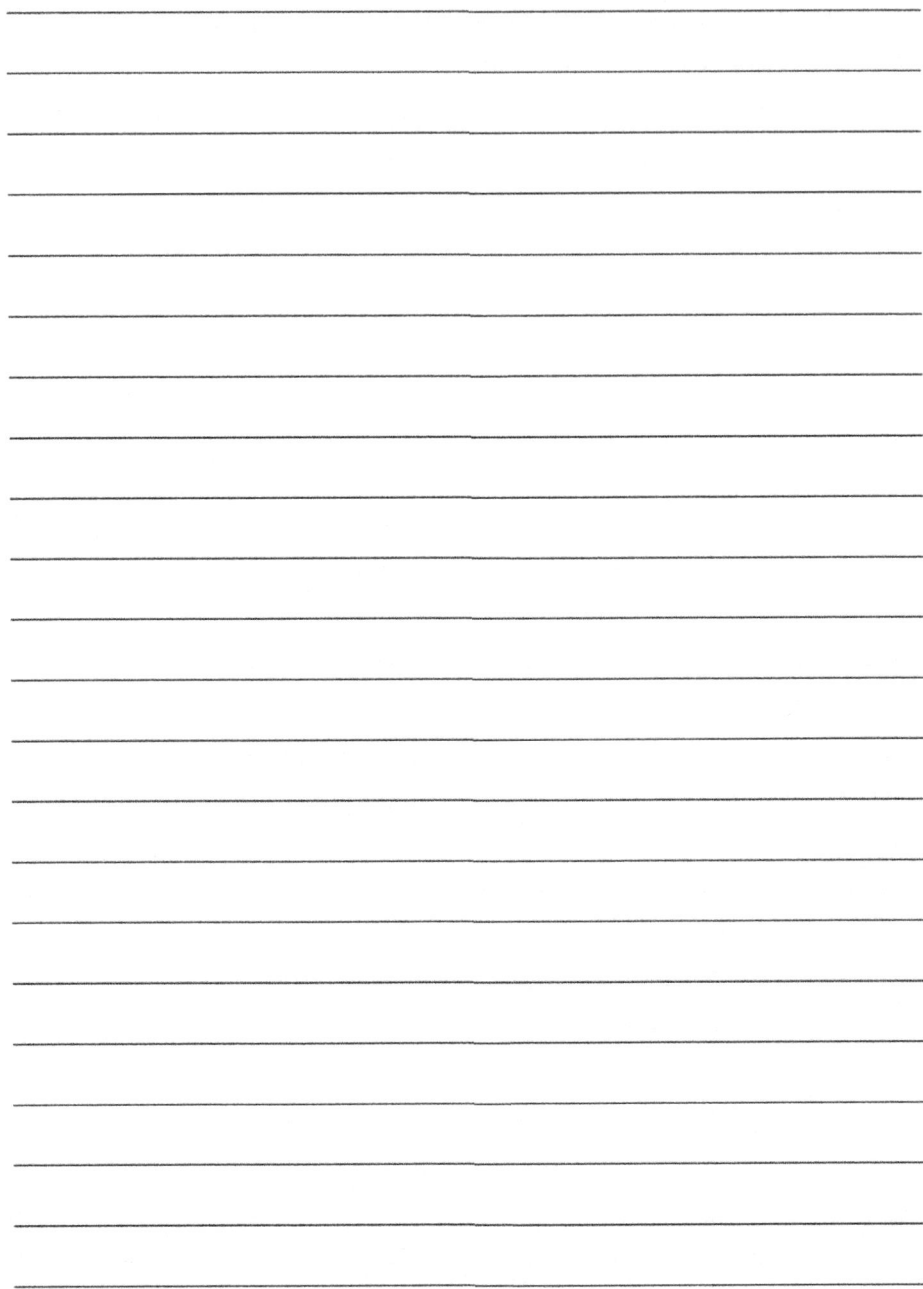

Write a letter to your inner child,
offering words of encouragement,
understanding, and love.

DATE _____

_____

_____

_____

_____

_____

_____

_____

_____

_____

_____

_____

_____

_____

_____

_____

_____

_____

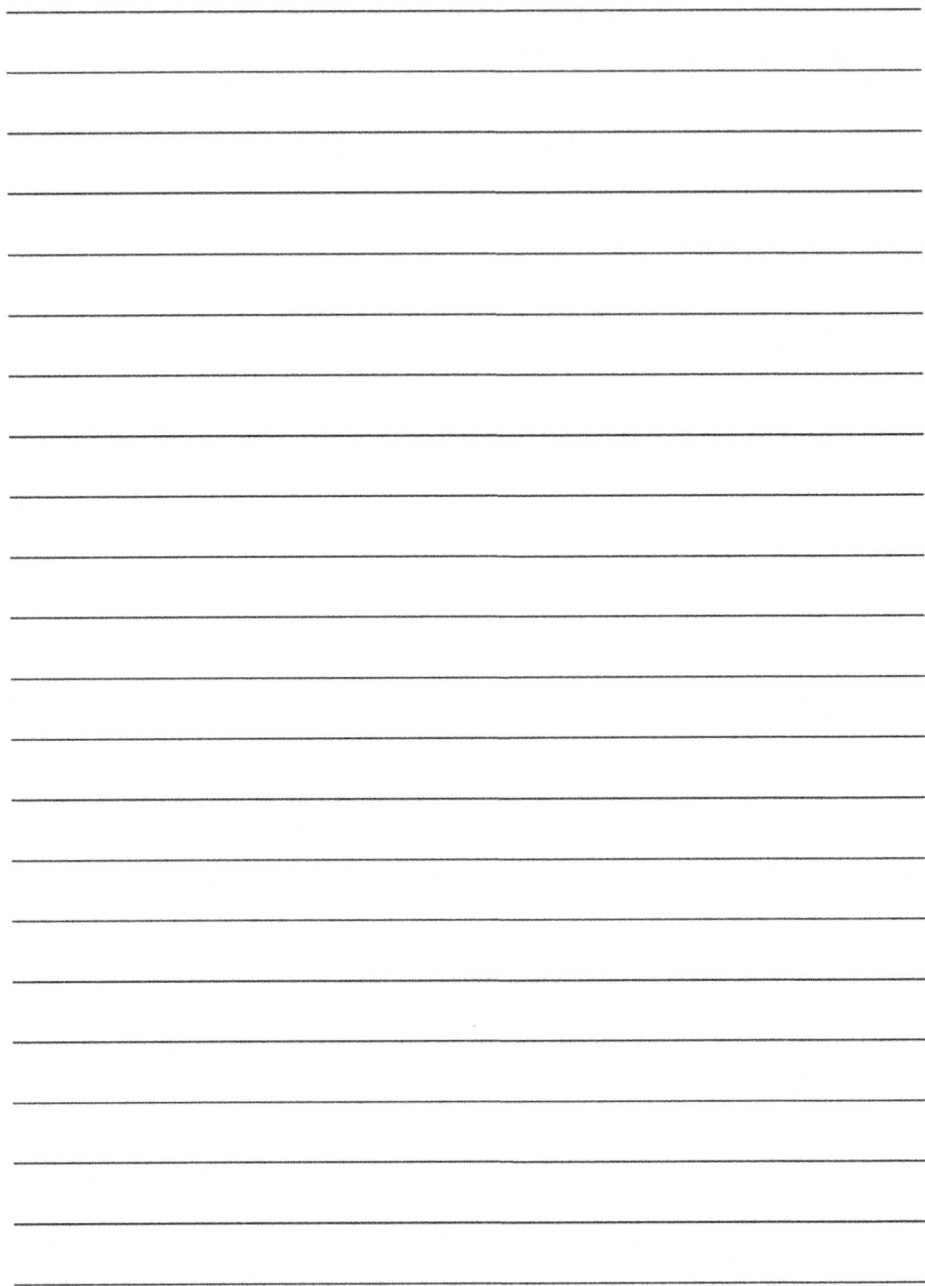

What do you think about social media? How does it make you feel? Do you think taking a digital detox from time to time is important?

DATE _____

_____

_____

_____

_____

_____

_____

_____

_____

_____

_____

_____

_____

_____

_____

_____

_____

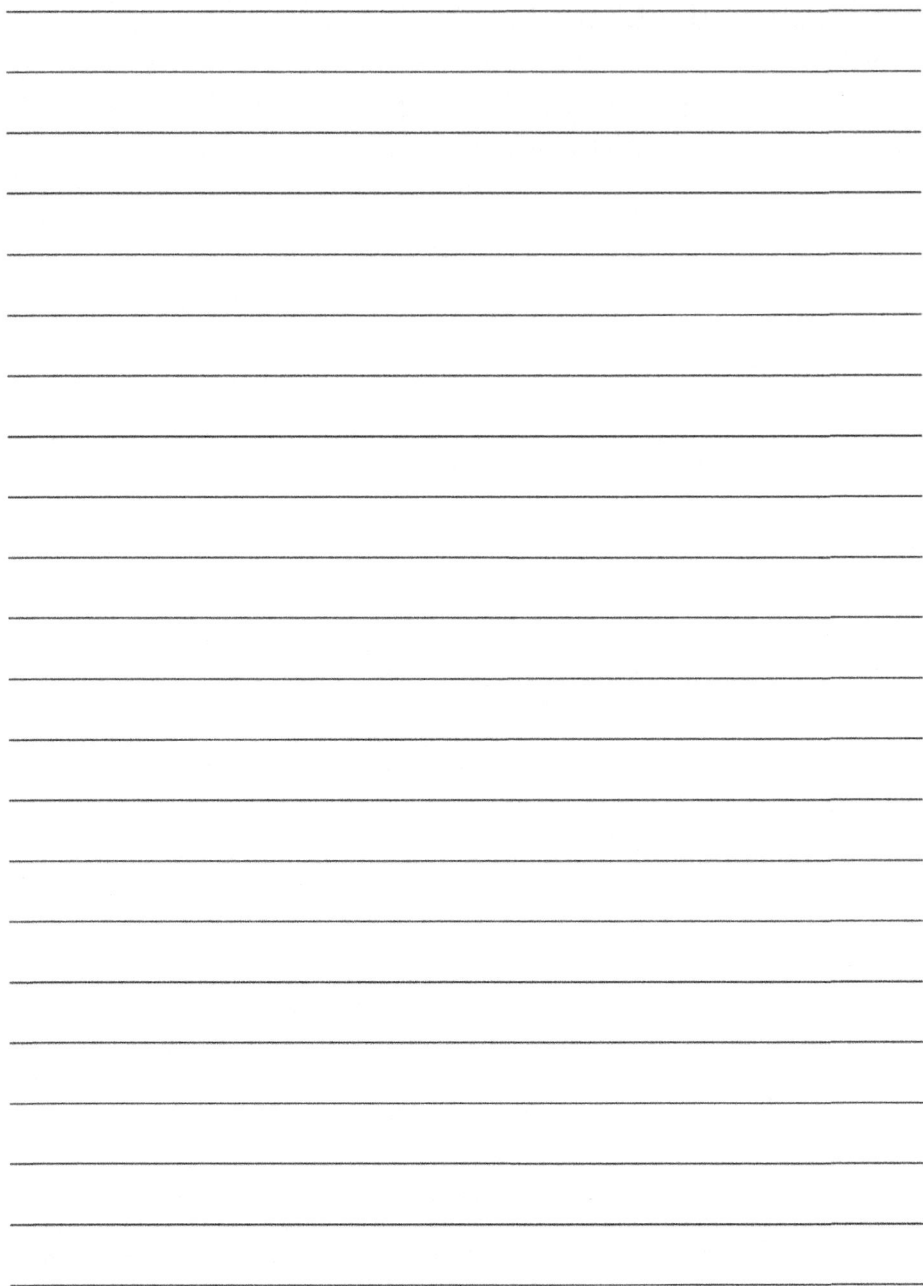

List one person who has believed in you. Why is this person special to you, and what are three nice things you can do for yourself today?

DATE _____

_____

_____

_____

_____

_____

_____

_____

_____

_____

_____

_____

_____

_____

_____

_____

_____

_____

_____

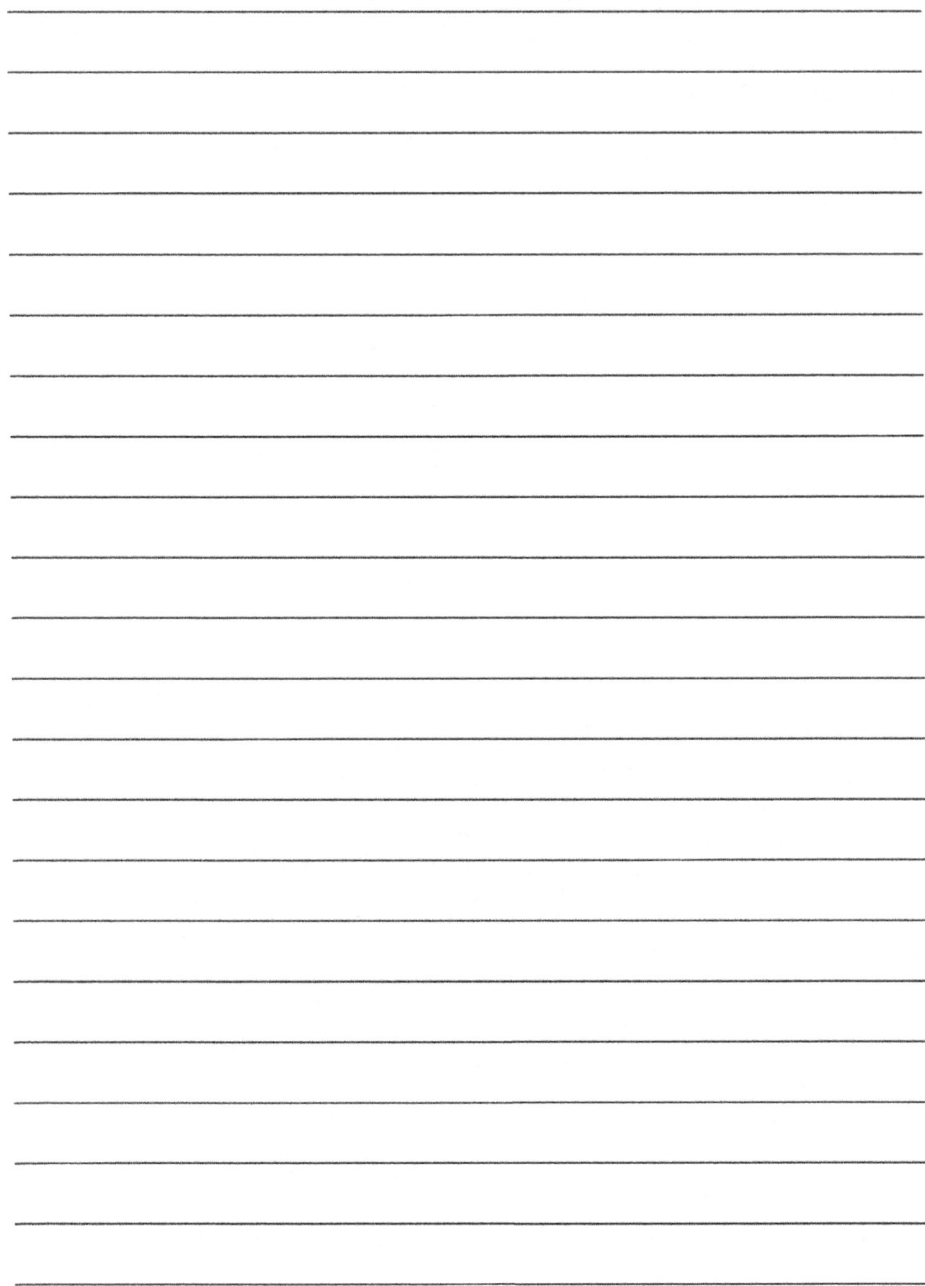

How do you define happiness and contentment?

_____

_____

_____

_____

_____

_____

_____

_____

_____

_____

_____

_____

_____

_____

_____

_____

_____

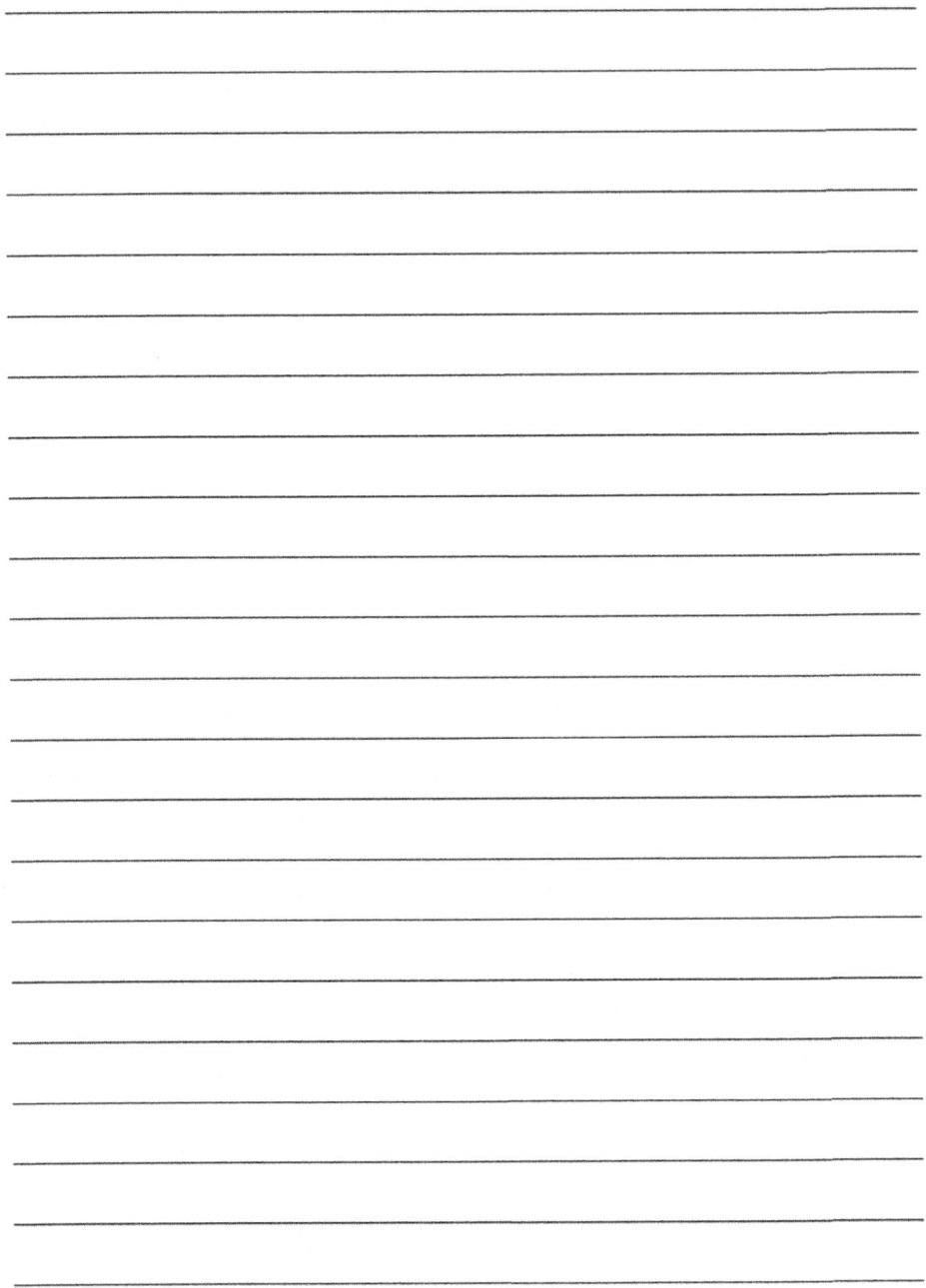

L is for Love

Love is _Kind_

Love is

Love is

Love is

Love is

Write any words you want...

Write about a fear that you're ready
to overcome, why it exists, and one
way you can get started to
release it.

_____

_____

_____

_____

_____

_____

_____

_____

_____

_____

_____

_____

_____

_____

_____

_____

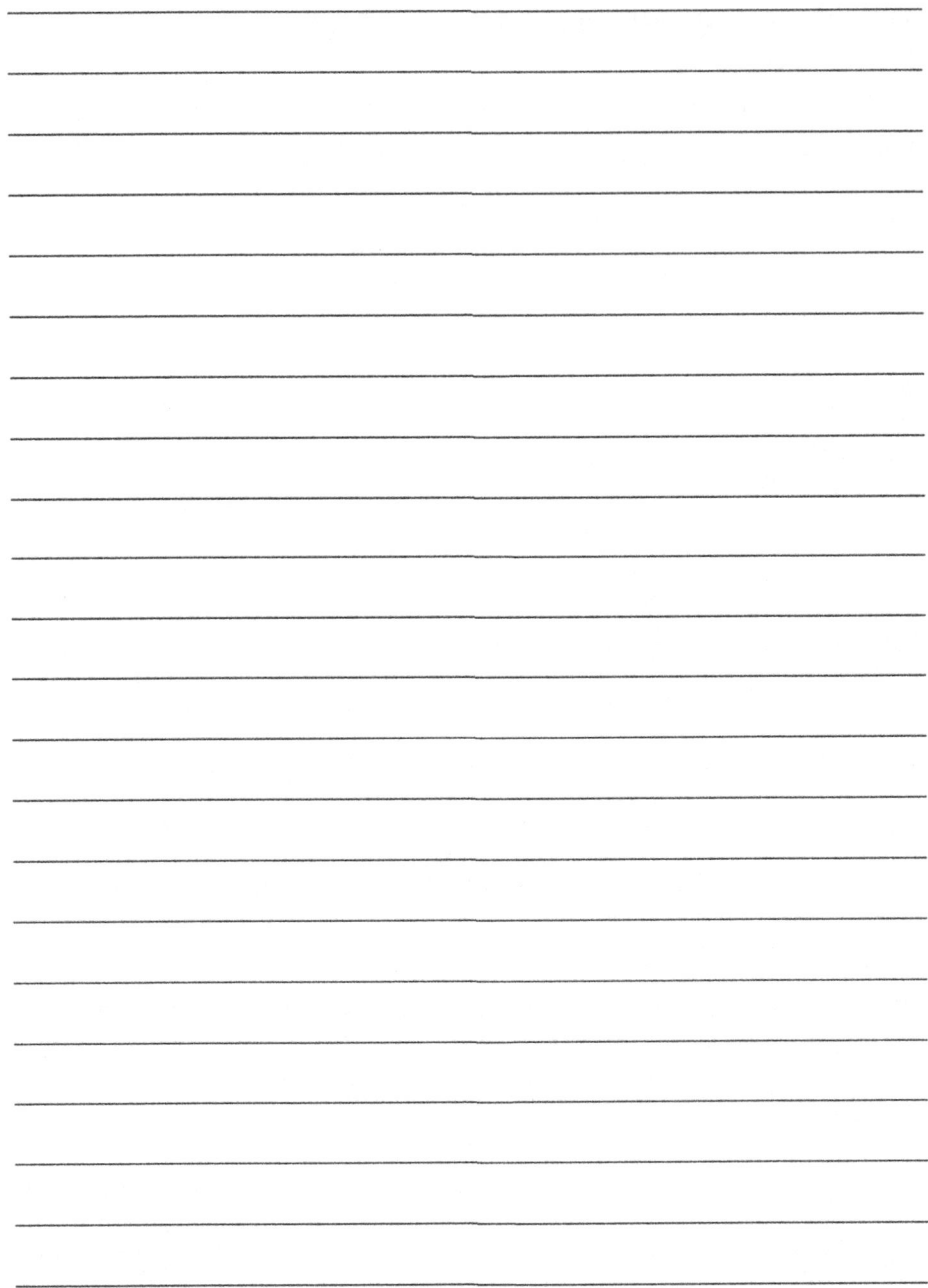

What does community mean to you? Describe the community or communities you feel connected to.

DATE _____

_____

_____

_____

_____

_____

_____

_____

_____

_____

_____

_____

_____

_____

_____

_____

_____

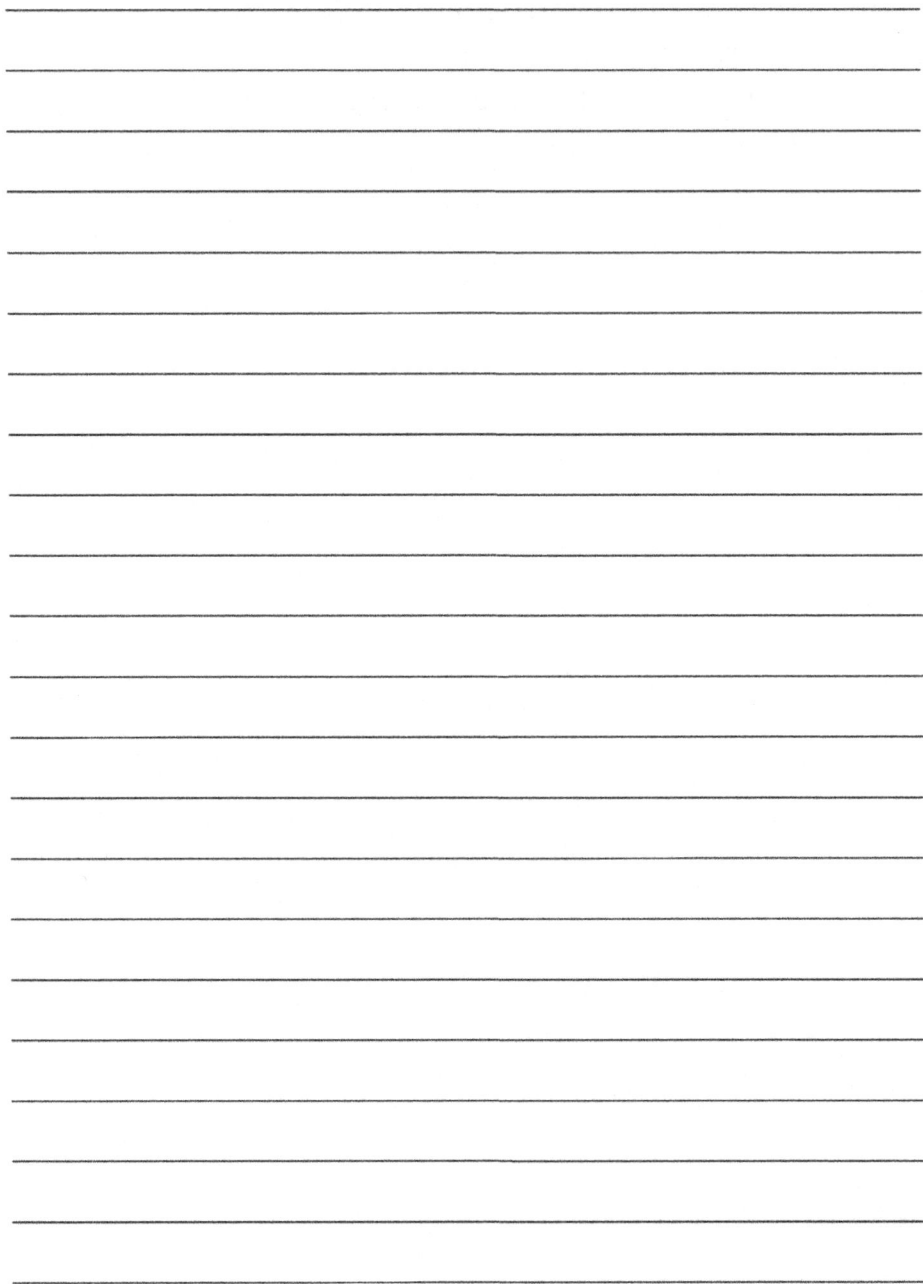

Reflect on the impact you wish to make in your community. What small steps can you take today to begin this journey of giving back?

_____

_____

_____

_____

_____

_____

_____

_____

_____

_____

_____

_____

_____

_____

_____

_____

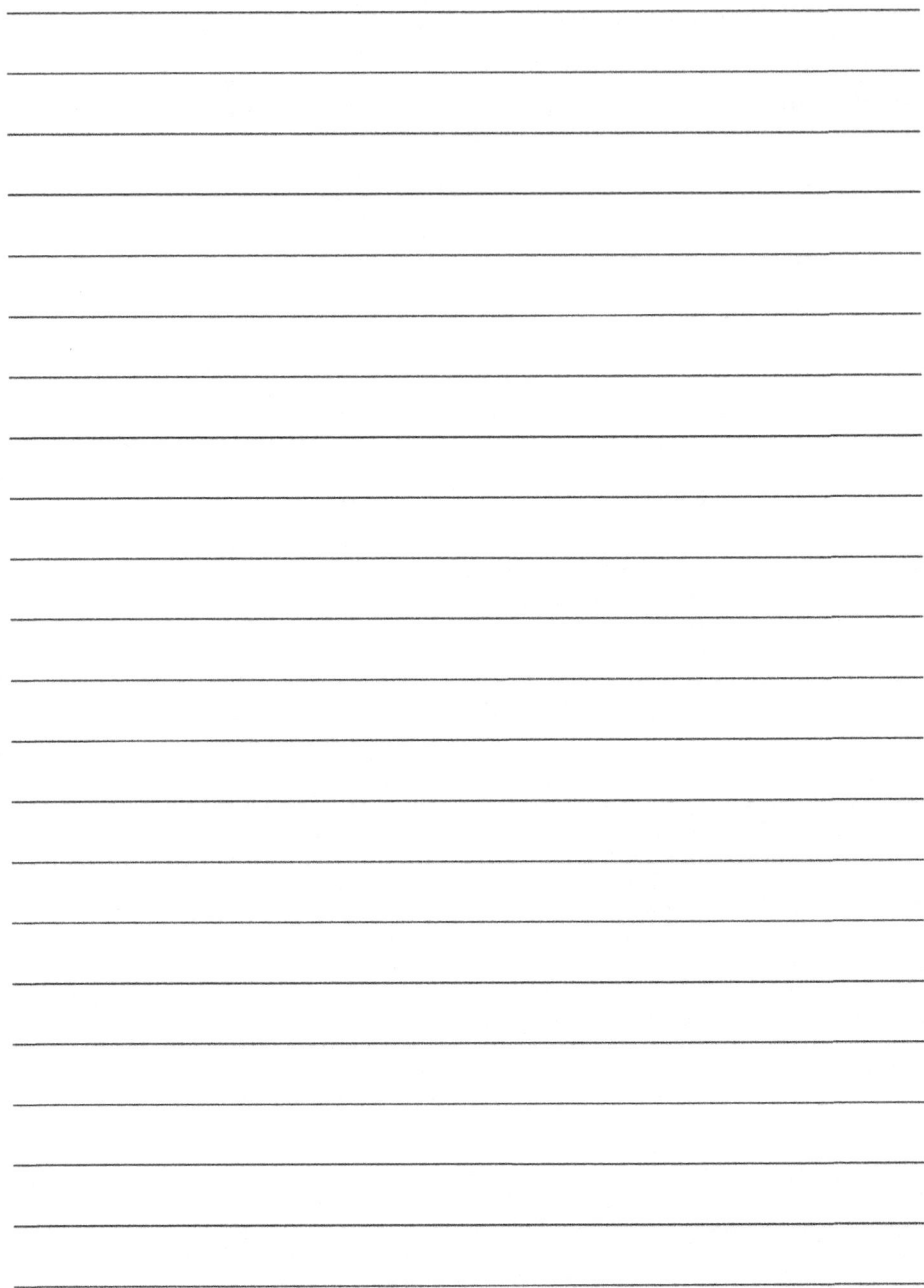

How do you plan to measure your progress on the path to self-love? In what ways can you celebrate your progress?

DATE _____

_____

_____

_____

_____

_____

_____

_____

_____

_____

_____

_____

_____

_____

_____

_____

_____

_____

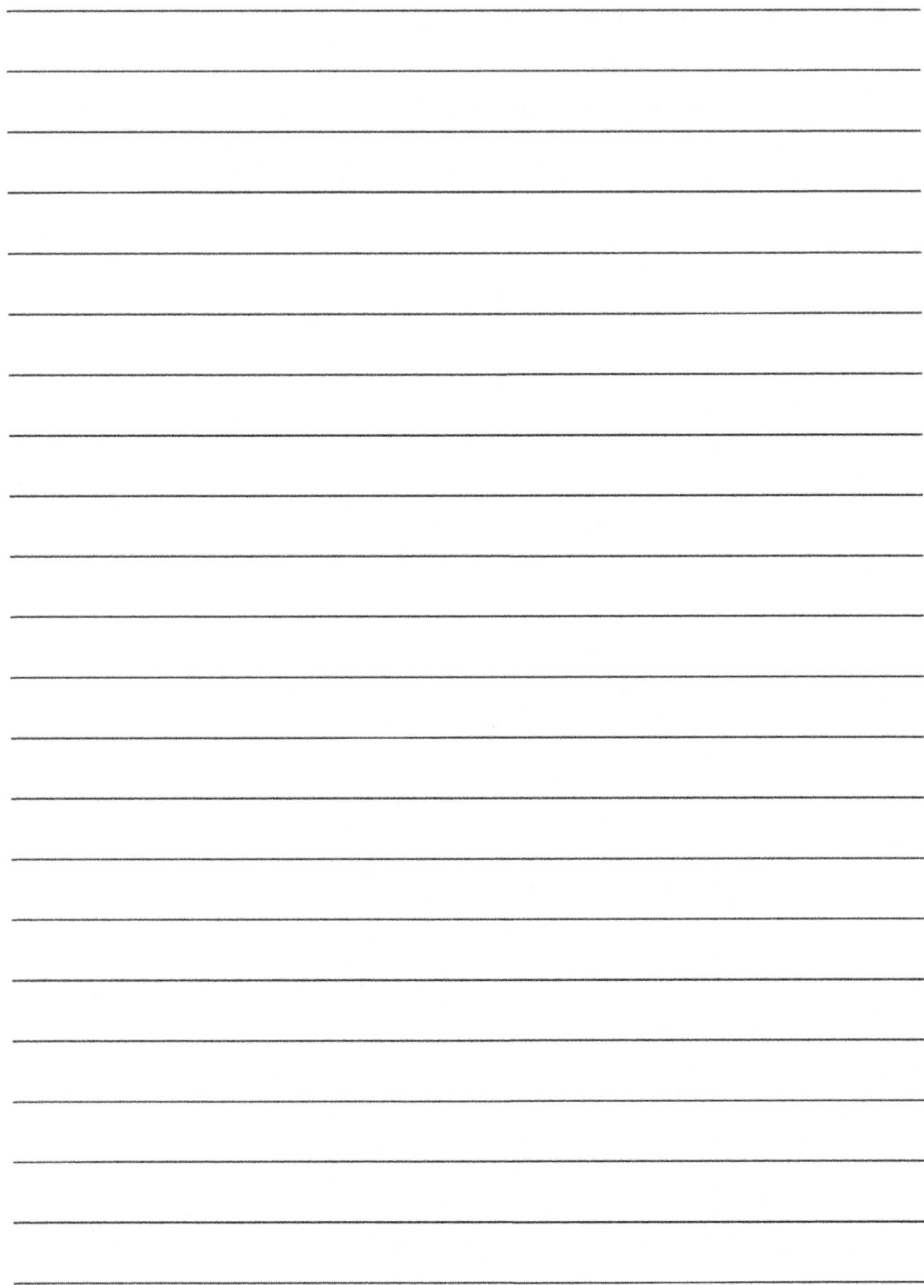

Describe the ideal version of
yourself and how you can work
toward becoming that person.   DATE _____

_____

_____

_____

_____

_____

_____

_____

_____

_____

_____

_____

_____

_____

_____

_____

_____

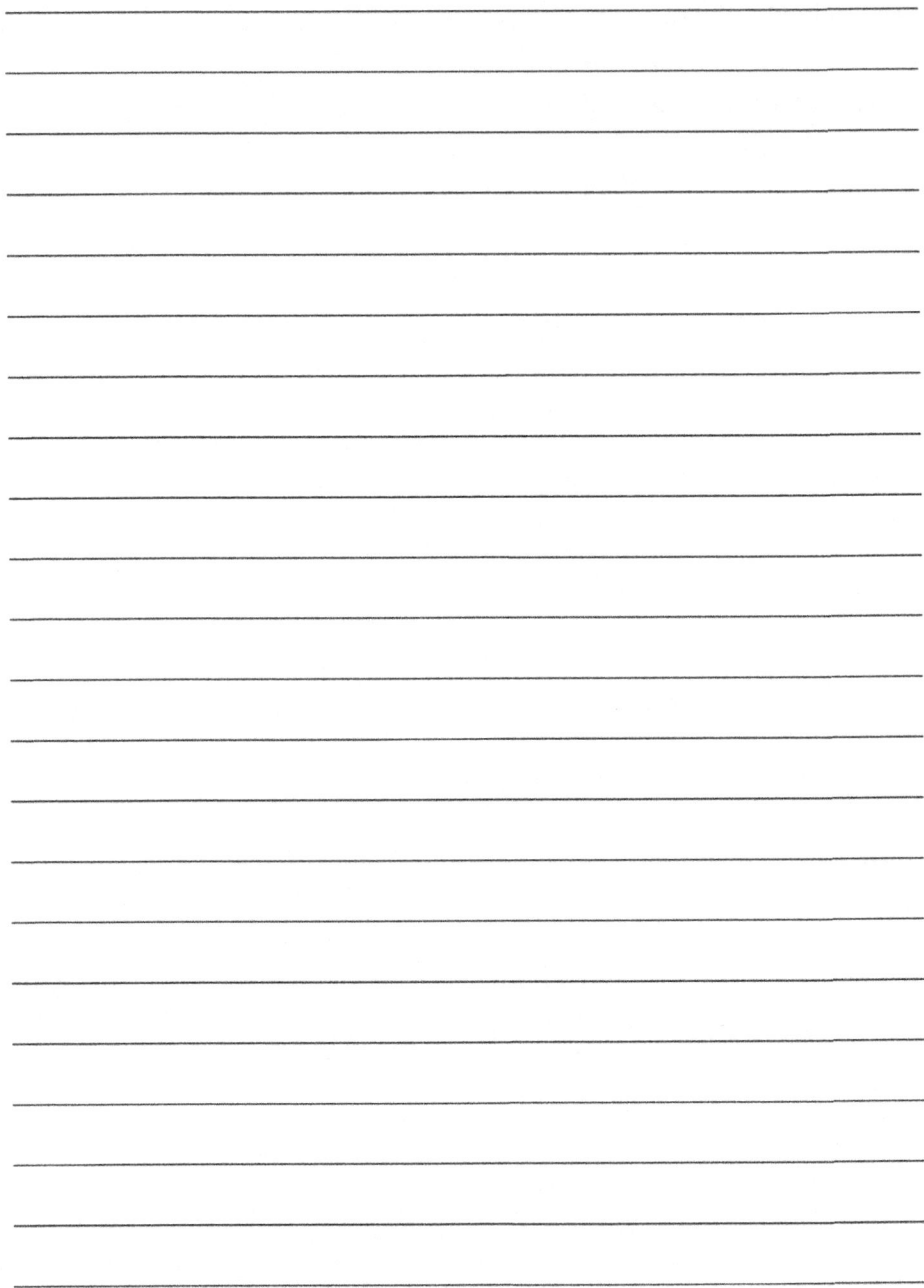

What's important in a healthy home?

What makes your spirit
feel nourished?

Notes...

Made in the USA
Middletown, DE
02 July 2024

56700242R00091